Church, Science, and a Rabbit:

An Amiable Conflict

Church, Science, and a Rabbit:

An Amiable Conflict

Charles Sigman, OSL

iUniverse, Inc.
New York   Bloomington

Church, Science, and a Rabbit: An Amiable Conflict

iUniverse books may be ordered through booksellers or by contacting:

iUniverse
1663 Liberty Drive
Bloomington, IN 47403
www.iuniverse.com
1-800-Authors (1-800-288-4677)

Because of the dynamic nature of the Internet, any Web addresses or links contained in this book may have changed since publication and may no longer be valid. The views expressed in this work are solely those of the author and do not necessarily reflect the views of the publisher, and the publisher hereby disclaims any responsibility for them.

ISBN: 978-1-4401-5768-4 (pbk)
ISBN: 978-1-4401-5769-1 (ebk)

Printed in the United States of America

iUniverse rev. date: 7/9/2009

Contents

Introduction

This project started in August of 1991 as strictly a literary endeavor focusing on the writings of John Updike, specifically his four "Rabbit" novels: *Rabbit, Run, Rabbit Redux, Rabbit Is Rich*, and *Rabbit At Rest*. Within these novels, Updike, who is perhaps as much of a historian of modernity as he is a writer, presents bits and pieces of reflection on the impact science and technology has had upon humanity which in turn has a direct affect upon the Church. The main character, Rabbit, is given such a name because he is of the earth. Updike traces Rabbit's development through the decades, and the reader is given a vision on how much science and technology can separate us from what it means to be human.

After writing an essay on this subject, I put the Updike materials away, but because of Updike's vision and inspiration, I started collecting essays and articles over the years addressing the cultural impact of science in the 20th and 21st centuries upon American culture. With each passing year since 1991, the intervals between technological advancements or development, shortened. What once took years, especially when it comes to personal computers and smart phones, for new developments and subsequent availability now takes days and weeks. There probably have been more technological improvements to the cellular phone in the last year than the previous ten years combined.

In June of 1996, I entered the ministry in the United Methodist Church. Right away, I was baptized by Church leaders into their fears of what to do about an aging and declining Methodist denomination. Workshop after workshop provided so-called tools for turning the denomination's decline around. Clergy were given a list of ten-steps-to-success books to read and models to emulate. However, no matter the reading lists, the workshops, and the guest speakers, no one for me has adequately tackled the question: Why is this decline happening to mostly the mainline, Protestant churches? However, no matter the reading lists, the workshops, and the guest speakers, no one adequately tackled the question: Why is this decline happening to the mainline, Protestant churches only? Top ten lists of various approaches to take do not answer that question. Until the Church can get to the heart of the problem, for me it is about culture relevancy in a technological world, the decline will persist. How can there be a cure if no one knows the disease? The disease plaguing the Church is cultural irrelevancy, which is effecting all denominations at different rates, even the mega, non-denominational churches are not immune from this plague.

This book is about the conflict between science/technology and the Church/religion, in the postmodern world. I use the Church as the religious paradigm because it remains the dominant form of worship in the West, especially the United States. But Christianity's stronghold is lessening. Fewer and fewer people are claiming Christian affiliation. As a whole, church membership and worship attendance are dropping. Part of the problem is that science and technology are more relevant to today's generation than the Church. Communities of blogging, text messaging, chat rooms, and so on are replacing after worship pot-luck meals and other social gatherings for fellowship. Flesh and blood community is replaced by computer chips, smart phones, and wireless cafes. These items are not bad in themselves. In fact, they are wonderful tools for making life better for people. Unfortunately, these "tools" are bringing about greater distance between the "haves" and the "have-nots," and they are creating greater distance between people in general.

Face-to-face contact allows people to read body language and facial expressions. In other words, one can be speaking sarcastically and based on the facial expression of the other, one knows rather the sarcasm is understood or not. One can send a good friend a sarcastic email, and have that email misinterpreted resulting in the end of a friendship. Personal emails, photos, and text messages may accidentally be sent out to a hundred people.

Over the last fifteen years of my ministry I have seen both the positives and negatives of technology. For the most part, technology has made lives better, but when technology drives humanity and when science defines the human condition, problems arise. One such problem is science has the potential for destroying myth. Myth is the thread that holds the human tapestry or narrative together. One role the Church must take on is to keep science and technology in their proper place by saying, "No," when the two overstep their limitations. Currently, there are no checks and balances placed upon science. Science is accountable to no one but itself. Humans are imperfect, and thus, science is imperfect. In this way, the Church brings meaning and purpose to religion, while still affirming science's role of making people's physical lives better. Both science and religion need a level of utilitarian mission, purpose, and vision. The Church and science must be in a friendly, adversarial relationship. Conflict is good and healthy because from out of conflict comes great creativity. Adversity spawns creativity. When science and religion are in healthy, amiable conflict, creativity emerges—just as the butterfly struggles to emerge from the cocoon.

Chapter 1: The Event Horizon

Yet we seek to impose patterns of meaning around ourselves, interlocking
networks vectored back to the ego, le point de depart, if not the
Archimedean Point that lifts this heavy, tangled, cluttered world into
schematic form we can manipulate (Villages, 308).

In the April 13, 2009 issue of *Newsweek* magazine, R. Albert Mohler, Jr. was cited as saying, "'A remarkable culture-shift has taken place around us,' Mohler said." "'The most basic contours of American culture have been radically altered. The so-called Judeo-Christian consensus of the last millennium has given way to a postmodern, post-Christian, post-Western cultural crisis which threatens the very heart of our culture.'" He goes on to say that, "'clearly, there is a new narrative, a post-Christian narrative, that is animating large portions of society'" (Meacham, 34). What has created this scenario? The infiltration of science and technology in all parts of society is perhaps the culprit. Technology is now the new narrative by providing answers to the mysterious of life, and by altering the way we live.

Science and technology in the hands of greed and the military industrial complex has a potential for disaster. Likewise, religion embraced by fanatics is equally ruinous. The two must co-exist. One should not absorb or co-opt the other because it is essential for science and church or religion to remain in an amiable conflict. This allows for checks and balances. A movie was released in 2007 called, *I am Legend*—a remake of two previous movies most notably is the *Omega Man* starring Charleston Heston. The premise of the movie involved the development of a genetically-engineered virus initially intended for medical purposes. The virus in the hands of the military left the confines of the laboratory killing the people who were unable to escape. Those who could not leave were turned into flesh-eating creatures confined to the shadows of night and avoiding the light of day.

The virus had altruistic beginnings. Scientists were looking for a cure for cancer, and their research led them to genetically alter the measles virus to attack cancer cells. Of course, the military industrial complex grabbed the technology for its own purposes. The military turned it into a weapon, and unfortunately for humanity, the virus mutated resulting in the apparent destruction of humanity with the exception of the Omega Man. Toward the end of the movie he finds another survivor, a woman, who was able to find an outpost of survivors. Life goes on. Did science in the hands of the military go too far? Yes it did, but at the conclusion of the movie and in Christ-like imagery, it was the death of one man whose body and blood brought salvation to the world because his blood contained the antibodies. It was one man's sacrifice that ended what science and technology had started. He gave himself over to the flesh-eating creatures, saving them by his blood. In sum, it took the sacrifice of one man in order for humanity to reclaim its identity. Humanity saved humanity not the science that causes the outbreak in the first place. Science could not do it. Science and technology have brought great good to the world. The potential and actual benefits can be felt in all areas of human life, but just as science and technology have the potential for great good they also possess the potential for great evil. There exists the potential for great destruction when technology is placed in the wrong hands. North Korea has challenged the West by demonstrating its use of technology through its development of a nuclear weapon with long range capacity. Every Christian church in the world should unilaterally give a resounding, "No," to North Korea. Yet, collectively, the Church remains silent.

Interestingly, throughout the movie several teenage girls were constantly sending out text messages, and every fifteen minutes or so they had to have the movie explained to them. Society has moved from teenage bantering and giggling during a movie to a sort of techno-community evident by the barrage of text messaging during the movie. Technology is present in all aspects of society, and the Church is no exception. One must ask, what is the Church's place within this scientific world that has given birth to technologies influencing every aspect of life? Ironically, the Church was the dominant institution for centuries infiltrating and controlling all areas of society, answering life's questions. That role is slowly being replaced by science.

The churches of Europe and North America (Europe being farther along) are in their *Event Horizon* (a state of diminishment leading to its destruction) which contributes to and also explains the decline in the mainline Protestant churches since the 1970s—corresponding to the greatest ongoing period of scientific achievement and discovery as well as technological advancement ever seen from putting a man on the moon to genetic mapping. The *Event Horizon* is the outer rim of a black hole that pulls all matter and energy into the vortex where it is destroyed. The churches of the Third World, unfortunately, which have shown considerable growth throughout the 1990s and 2000s, will eventually experience this same decline. At some point, technology will reach the Third World. Episcopalians, Methodists, Pentecostals, Presbyterians, and so forth are all reporting rapid growth in places like Africa, South America, and South Korea. This growth-event is occurring because the average man and woman in the Third World are far from having access to science and technology, such as cellular phones, DVD players, world-wide internet, and so on—like those of the West. Technology has not yet replaced God, but the more technology and the greater scientific advancements mean the lesser the need for God.

The ecumenical officer for the Council of Bishops of the United Methodist Church reported that a major shift is underway in its ecumenical and Methodist relations "due to the dramatic growth in churches overseas" (Arkansas-Democrat, 4B). This is in reference to the general growth of Methodism in the Third World.

Methodist Bishop William Oden said, "'we are entering a new phase that the Church has not encountered before because of globalization. Old borders and old agreements ... denominational and ecumenical, no longer hold'" (Arkansas-Democrat, 4B).

Putting denominational and polity issues aside, the fact remains churches are growing in the Third World countries. However, and perhaps unfortunately, once technology is made available to all people of the Third World, Christianity and more than likely other religions such as Islam will decline as well. There is a reason why the Taliban and Al Qaeda limit access to Western technology. They do not want technology supplanting faith. A program exists where one buys a computer and passes a computer on to an impoverished child around the world. This is a worthy cause, and nations and/or individuals should not withhold technology from marginalized people because science does improve life, but there is a dark side to technology. Cellular phones and the internet are evangelism tools for science. It is thus important for the Western Church to develop a theological response to the ever-developing scientific/technological god of the West worshipped by millions. It is an issue of ecclesiastical relevancy in the 21st century.

Stephen Hawking and Carl Sagan's Deism have given way to atheism. Robert John Russell in his lecture in the *Woodstock Report* says, "Deism is gone, but atheism is alive and well" (Russell, 7). These are some harsh words of indictment against the role and influence of the Church and religion; but perhaps, a better explanation is one of apathy concerning the Church's inability to mount a theological response to the postmodern age because science and technology provide distractions. Science and technology have replaced the cross and altar for this generation. Science and technology now provide the relevant answers to the meaning and purpose of life. Computer software and downloads, and the World Wide Web have become the hymnals and bibles of modernity.

Currently, technology is slowly trickling down to the people in the Third World; this slow pace has some advantages because technology can be gradually worked into society without much cultural disruption. Technology in the U.S. and Europe is not a trickle, but a deluge.

This inundation has prevented a healthy integration of science and technology into Western society and culture, and so, the Church runs the risk of being swept away by the torrent.

In a local sandwich shop and café, there were clusters of people in clearly social groups. One particular group sat at a table with their laptop computers in front of them. They carried on a conversation while emailing and surfing the web. They had food and drinks by their side; in addition, another group sat with their cellular telephones text messaging people. These technological-based social groups have replaced the fellowship circles, the Sunday school classes, Bible study groups, and so forth. At one time, the Church provided the only social outlet for people, but those days are gone. Email is now the heart, the driving force of community, and technology now spawns community. It is important to note that it is not the Body of Christ under threat, but rather, the institutional church runs the risk of cultural and societal irreverence.

During a "Church Revitalization" workshop for Methodist clergy, the speaker addressed declining membership, and gave some reasons for the decline, and provided some ways to turn the decline into a climate of growth. California is a good example of the effect science and technology has on religion. A fellow clergyman in San Francisco revealed that his city is in a "post-Christian" era. San Francisco is nestled in the heart of technology. The guest speaker at the church growth workshops cited structural, organizational, and spiritual problems as the reason for the drop in numbers. His assessment was partially correct, but he missed the bigger picture, and that is, we are living in a science/technological-driven world. The speaker mentioned how the churches in California and the West Coast are small in comparison to the South and Midwest. California, i.e. Silicon Valley, is the technological capital of the United States. It is a Mecca for technology and science, so it is no surprise that the Church there is small and continues to shrink. The spiritual component is directly connected to technology.

Mainline protestant churches in fact are declining. For example, according to The General Committee on Archives and History, the United Methodist Church reported 10,671,774 members in the 1960s. Then, in 1970, the denomination reported 7,989,875 members which is a significant decline. The General Council on Finance and

Administration stated that the total attendance in the UMC has fallen to its lowest level ever at 3,344,743. The 1.05 percent decline in 2005 is the largest percentage of yearly decline for the UMC since 1975. The General Conference reported that if congregations continue to age and membership loss continues at its current pace, the United Methodist Church will shrink to the size at its inception during the Christmas Conference of 1784. Why are mainline, Protestant congregations aging? Why are young people not attending church? First, the Church is no longer relevant to their lives. The reality of sin and salvation mean nothing to a generation that rather text message than speak face to face. It is important to note that The United Methodist Church is not alone because other denominations run the risk of dying. All mainline churches are scrambling to reverse this trend by implementing various growth-based programs and by advertising believing these measures will stop the decline and reverse the downward momentum. Unfortunately, these attempts at renewal will not have any significant effect on current trends faced by institutional churches. Technology's challenge to religion and its rapid advancement will eventually effect the growth of the more evangelical, conservative churches as well. Amidst science's rapid advancement into all areas of life from entertainment to medicine, an important question must be asked: What is the relevancy of the Church? This is the fundamental question the Church must address in order to stop the hemorrhaging of Christianity. It all comes down to relevancy: cultural, spiritual, and social relevancy. Science and technology are seen as relevant today by younger generations. Blogging and chat rooms provide immediate gratification. So, can the Church articulate its relevancy to a technological, instant-gratification world? Church programs and advertising will not work until it is able to articulate a clear theological response to the world and to a rapidly changing society due to technology. Can the Church compete with instantaneous response and reward? The answer lies in authentic community, and the Church must communicate a viable and relative alternative.

Christianity represents about 34 percent of the world's population, and in North America about 75 percent of adults consider themselves Christian. These seem like positive numbers, but there is a real disconnect between calling oneself Christian and expressing that faith through worship attendance. The importance of religion has declined generally in the West, but the worship attendance in the United States remains far better than that in Europe. For the most part: 53 percent of Americans believe religion is important which compares to 16 percent in Britain, 14 percent in France, and 13 percent in Germany. There are, however, some disturbing trends in the United States. The percentage of American adults who call themselves Christian dropped from 86 percent in 1990 to 77 percent in 2001. This is an "unprecedented drop of almost 1 percentage point per year." Those who identify themselves as Protestants dropped below 50 percent in 2005. These trends follow a similar pattern to that of the European Christian landscape, except not as rapid. If this rate continues, most Americans will identify themselves as non-religious or non-Christian by the year 2035. More telling, confidence in religious institutions is at an all time low. Finally, the average worship attendance in 1992 was 102; it fell to 89 in 2003. As briefly touched upon, mainline denominations have been losing members for decades in the US; however, conservative denominations have shown some growth. The numbers for the Roman Catholic Church seem to remain stable (Religious Tolerance.Org,). The 2009 *Newsweek* article on the future of Christianity cites some disturbing figures as well. According to the American Religious Identification Survey, those who claim to be Christian had fallen from 86 percent to 76 percent since 1990. "A separate Pew Forum poll echoed the ARIS finding, reporting that the percentage of people who say they are unaffiliated with any particular faith has doubled in recent years, to 16 percent" (Meacham, 34).

The period of decline started in 1970, and it continues to this day, and all mainline denominations show similar trends. What has happened?

The answer is simple, and perhaps, Pope John Paul II said it best while addressing a group of scientists in 1985. He said previously, scientific discoveries effected humanity about every century or so. "Now they (discoveries) are made on much shorter timescales—every year, every month, even every week, and what is perhaps more significant, the impact of technology is almost immediate" (Pope John Paul II, 1985).

Science and technology are moving forward at an incredible rate.

Thus, the decline in worship numbers corresponds to the increase in available technologies. Pope John Paul II continues, "In fact, within the last few decades we have witnesses more basic advances in our understanding of physical reality than had been made during the entire previous history of our planet. There is strong evidence that this exponential growth will continue" (Pope John Paul II, 1985). So, what is the Church to do? How is it to respond? The future of the Church is bleak unless it can answer the previous two questions. Survival is dependant upon it. What is the Church to do? How should it respond?

The United Methodist Church is a good example of middle to upper class America, a denomination that has moved from working class to professional. This upward mobility means more access to technology. Methodists have more money, and thus, more purchasing power than denominations that attract the working class. For mainline denominations in general, technology is readily available. Is it such a coincidence that the rise and seemingly falling of Methodism [including mainline Protestant churches] corresponds to upward-class movement and the increased availability to technology? Anglican priest John Wesley, founder of the Methodist movement in the 18th Century, warned of the dangers of financial affluence. As Methodism moved from its lower and working class roots to a middle and upper class denomination and when one considers more money means greater access to technology, it is no coincidence that the decline of Methodism, as well as all mainline Protestant churches, is connected to technological development accessed solely by financial means. More money, more technology means more idolatry. The seeds of decline of the mainline churches were unknowingly planted after the development of the Atomic Bomb which threw America into the postmodern, scientific, and technological age. For better or for worse, technology began to solve life's problems. That, and the rapid economic advancement following World War II from working class to middle and upper class, gave people the economic power to purchase technology which really did not come into play until the late 1960s about the same time churches began to experience small decline. As science advanced and as technology become more available to people, church attendance and membership dropped nation wide during that same period and will continue to drop until the Church finds its own identity and relevancy in this technologically-driven world. One can surmise a direct correlation between the rise of science and the decline of the Church. Interestingly, the Amish population with its rejection of technology in Lancaster County, Pennsylvania has doubled over twenty years. It has been projected that at this rate there could be 480,000 Amish in Lancaster County before the year 2100, and perhaps even one million twenty years later (Igou, 1). These figures are questionable, but any growth in such a community means that some needs are being met.

The western Church is in its *Event Horizon*. The use of scientific language is intentional here because emphasis is needed to drive home the point that science is co-opting religion by now providing answers to the mysteries of existence. Science is co-opting the Church by making it less and less relevant to a generation that no longer communicates with a handshake and face-to-face conversation. The *Event Horizon* can be applied in many different ways in regards to general relativity, but the most common association of the *Event Horizon* is with black holes. The *Event Horizon* in very limited layman's terms is the periphery around a black hole, a sort of plane around the edge of a funnel. Within this horizon or periphery, matter and light are warped and pulled inevitably into the black hole where nothing can escape. The black hole's *Event Horizon* pulls matter and energy into its periphery and eventually into the black hole's center. If a black hole would pass close enough to the earth, our bodies would be pulled and stripped apart into smaller and smaller pieces until mere particles are left or nothing is left, depending on how one theorizes about black holes. The church is being pulled into oblivion, i.e. irrelevancy, by a science-driven world that has produced more technological advancements than at any time in history. Stephen Hawking's original theory suggested that all of matter and energy are gone within a black hole, but since his initial theories, subsequent physicists have re-interpreted it to mean matter and energy cannot be fully destroyed. There is always a remnant of it. Thus, if the Church is in the *Event Horizon*, the question must be ask if whether or not the Church as known today can reverse its current path toward complete irrelevancy, which could mean destruction. Or, can the Church reassemble itself, by means of another Reformation, or will the Church be sucked into irrelevancy and thus gone forever. Is there a remnant, like the Israelites in exile?

One does not have to look hard to see the pull of science upon faith. The language we use communicates much about who we are as individuals, as a culture, and as a people. Language communicates a powerful message about what it means to be human. For example, a common phrase these days used at church-growth workshops goes as follows, "the Church must have lay ministries as part of its *DNA*." Furthermore, one often hears the phrase, "evolution of the church." Perhaps, a better choice of words would be the "revelation for the Church." This would suggest an outside force influencing the Church rather than an internal mechanism of growth. When we say "evolution" of the Church we risk removing God from the equation. Also, in evolutionary models, there are winners and losers. It is opposite of Christ's teachings. Pope John Paul himself co-opted scientific language into church language. After praising science for recent discoveries into the nature of the universe, he said, " ...you and others around the world are perfecting a model which traces the whole evolution of the universe from an infinitesimal instant after the starting point of time up to the present, and beyond, into the distant future" (Pope John Paul, 1997). He, too, uses words like "evolution" as part of his theological vocabulary. There should be no doubt that certain fish moved out of the water and onto the land and became land dwellers. The evolutionary process is far from perfect, so why use an imperfect model to describe God's work on earth. There is nothing wrong with evolution when it is kept within its proper scientific boundaries. Even socio-evolution has its problems because of the element of chaos that human beings bring to the world. The Pope's use of "evolution" only shows how much science has become part of Church vocabulary, and how it has permeated our culture. Pope John Paul opened the door to this question: Is Christ the Perfector of the world or is it evolution or is it science?

Another way the Church is pulled into the *Event Horizon* occurs when faith engages science on science's turf such as when people of faith try to use science to prove the existence of God, or God's actions such as parting the Red Sea. Ironically, as mentioned earlier, Christians have incorporated evolution into its doctrine. Some will say, "How do you know God did not use evolution to create the world?" This diminishes the creative power of God. Evolution is about adaptation and moving genes into the future. To incorporate an evolutionary understanding of Creation into faith loses sight of the goodness of the Creator and the traces of God's beauty in all things. Creation and evolution must be kept apart and held in conflict with each other. Creation is not about how things came into being. It is about why things came into being, and it gives insight into the nature of God, a God who is creative and continues to create. Science challenges people of faith to prove God based upon observable or recordable phenomenon. People of faith are lured into using scientific tools and methods to prove matters of faith. How can such proof be when the existence of God is both of this world and not of this world? God, by definition, defies science by occupying multiple points in space and time. When ask to use scientific principles to prove God, the church walks right into that trap. Fundamentalists are vulnerable to this because they want scientific proof, so they try to prove the existence of God by stepping into that trap by applying scientific principles to prove, for example, that the world is only seven thousand years old, or by claiming there is evidence of an ancient, cataclysmic flood as described by the story of Noah in the Book of Genesis and other such examples. When proof becomes science-based rather than faith-based, and when science becomes the approach for answering questions of faith, the Church will surely lose its relevancy. Why go to Church for answers when one can go directly to the source—science? The Church will lose every time when it uses science to justify itself or to prove whether God exists or not. For every scientific-supported claim made by those who employ science to religion, there are always counter claims to be made. Faith must stand on its own merit to have validity and relevancy.

According to theologian and ethicist Stanley Hauerwas, if the Church could provide the kind of evidence as required by the scientific method in order to prove God's existence for those who want such evidence, then, the God as worshiped by Christians would not exist (Hauerwas, 29). God cannot be observed, nor can God be evidenced. God cannot be fully known by the observable world. Natural theology has created problems for the church of the 21st Century. Knowledge of God, according to Natural theology, comes by human reason and

observation: one can arrive at religious truths by thought. This approach
or understanding was rejected by the Reformed theologians, such as
John Calvin, who believed evidence cannot be gathered on God. The
observable world can provide mere glimpses of the Divine. The Apostle
Paul in his letter to the church at Rome states, "For the wrath of God
is revealed from heaven against all ungodliness and wickedness ..."
(Romans 1:18). This is in line with Revealed Theology which states
that only by divine revelation from God are we given insight into God.
This is in opposition to science and Natural Theology. Paul goes on
to write, "Ever since the creation of the world his eternal power and
divine nature, invisible though they are, have been understood and seen
through the things he has made" (Romans 1:20). Paul is not referring
to observing God in nature and thus knowing God. The Divine nature
is made known through God's interaction with humanity. The glimpses
we get of God happen through God's grace directed toward humanity
or God's children including God's wrath toward sin. The Church
needs to withdraw from the need to prove itself to science by using
scientific principles, and spend its time focusing more on the struggles
of humanity and its search for meaning in the present. The Church
must believe in God's perfecting of Creation for a better future.

There is a danger of focusing solely on humanity and not on
the Divine while in the meantime completely abandoning Creation
to science. Immanuel Kant's influence upon Christian theologians
essentially led to the handing over of the natural world to the realm
of science. This reduces religion to being a school of ethics. Christian
ethics without regard for Creation limits God's actions in the world.
Any Christian-based ethics must include the natural order (Hauerwas,
37-38). Twentieth Century theologian Karl Barth believed that there
must be some kind of direct encounter between God and humanity in
order for direct revelation to be intelligible and relevant. By being solely
concerned with ethics, as Kant pointed out, the paradoxical nature of
God is overlooked—God both condemns and loves. God in Christ is
both human and God, etc. God is completely "other" or "alien," so
because of these paradoxes and complete otherness, ethical behavior
can also be paradoxical which leads to conflict within religious faith.
For example, the debate over the right for one to choose to die because
one suffers from a non-curable, catastrophic illness or injury is not a

cut and dry ethical issue. In this case there are clear ethical conflicts, and these conflicts are not easily resolved. To die or not to die raises legitimate arguments on both sides. This is an issue in which conflict arises between faith and science as well as differing theologies. This is good because from out of this conflict, better understanding can come to light.

On the other hand, the fight between Creationist/Intelligent Design and Evolution is a debate that should not be happening. The school board in Dover, Pennsylvania that voted in 2005 to include intelligent design in ninth grade biology curriculum as an alternative should not have happened because it diminishes God. Since then, the decision was overturned. The Church is currently choosing the wrong battles to fight. The true battlefield is not over who made what or how things happen to come about; the true battle is of an existential nature. In his Nobel Peace Prize for Literature speech, southern author William Faulkner said the only battle worth fighting is the war within the human heart.

However, before proceeding, let's put all this in a brief, historical context. This is by no means intended to be all encompassing. The following describes a theological timeline leading up to where the Church is today. As you will see, unlike science where knowledge builds upon knowledge, theology has been all over the radar screen, and the theological history of the Church is one developed out of a response to issues of the day. How, then, is the Church theologically responding to our technologically-driven culture and society? There are some basic core beliefs as described by various creeds, but from that original orthodoxy, Christianity has grown in various directions. The following will show how Christianity has changed its theological understanding of God. As you will see, unlike science, theology does not necessarily build upon itself throughout the ages.

A good beginning is Saint Augustine (c. 354-430), for he is the first major theologian on the scene following the Apostle Paul to have a significant impact on Christian doctrine and theology. He leads Christianity into a new direction. Augustine did not have an interest in examining natural phenomenon. For him, all of the created order pointed toward the Creator—the glory surrounding all of us pointing toward something beyond itself and that is God. Augustine, however, did see the usefulness of reason and logic as long as they did not supersede faith. Faith must come first. Augustine's influence on faith abides in his understanding of Christian truth. He entered into conflict with the heresies of his time, and out of this conflict, his own theology was formulated. Later, we will see how the conflict between technology and religion or faith can bring about clarity of thought and purpose. Thus, conflict is good; it has its benefits.

Augustine put forth the understanding that God was the sole creator and sustainer of all things. Evil, then, is the deprivation of good, and this deprivation happens due to the imperfect character of God's creatures. Moral evil springs forth from humanity's acting out of free will. However, free will opens the flood gates for chaos.

Saint Albertus Magnus (c. 1200-1280) was crudely the first to begin thinking theologically, scientifically (based on the science of the times), and philosophically. Later in 1980, Pope John Paul II, while citing the contributions of Albertus, called for a dialogue between science and the Church. Albertus' writings were often unsystematic and somewhat contradictory; however, it was his teachings and writings that gave birth to Saint Thomas Aquinas, his pupil, who far exceeded his teacher.

Albertus, who was influenced by Jewish and Arabic writers as well as Aristotle and Augustinian schools of thought, was very knowledgeable despite his shortcomings as a writer. He did, however, foreshadow Aquinas' fusion of philosophy, science, and theology. He attempted, through his knowledge and strength of observation, to reform the sciences of his day, but his writings, which were problematic in form, unity, and fluidity, failed at this attempt. Only his pupil Aquinas could take on this task. For his love of wisdom and knowledge, Pope John Paul II defined him as *doctor of universalis* (Pope John Paul II, 1980, 1). He was beatified in 1622, and proclaimed *doctor ecclesiae* (church) in 1931 by Pious XI.

John Paul II described him as one challenging the intellectual discourse of the time by introducing comprehensive views of the world that went beyond Christianity while at the same time including it. For his time, according to John Paul II, Albert took a centrist position bringing together Christian tradition and radicals who saw "an unsolvable conflict between science rationality and truth of faith" (Pope John Paul, 1980, 2). As will be shown later, this is part of the problem when technology and religion encounter each other. In sum, Albert believed faith and science belong to different orders of knowledge. Science cannot arrive at knowledge which conflicts with the truth of faith. Thus, early in the middle age we begin to see the conflict between science and faith that remains into the 21st century Western Church.

Albert's pupil, St. Thomas Aquinas (c.1225-74), is the theological bulwark of the middle age as well as throughout the centuries even to this day. However, bulwark may be an inappropriate noun to use because it might have been Aquinas, this theological champion, who cracked opened the door for the decline of 21st Christianity in the West with its empty and mighty cathedrals. His attempt at reconciling philosophy and science with faith might have been the kiss of death, the betrayal of the Church.

Aquinas, attracted to the intellectual apostolate, resolved to become part of the Dominican Order in 1244, and it was Albert who introduced Aquinas to Aristotle which became an obvious influence on Aquinas' future writings. Interestingly, the Franciscan Order for a time kept its members from studying his works. Did the Franciscan Order sense the possible dangers that this Dominican might have introduced? Aquinas had a long history of intellectual pursuits from lecturing and teaching to writing. The extent of Aquinas' writings and teachings is so immense that it cannot be fully addressed here. However every attempt will be made in order to put him in a theological time frame leading up to the current theological state of affairs in the United States, specifically, and in the West generally.

Much of his theology and spirituality can be gleaned from his commentaries on the gospels, epistles, Isaiah, Jeremiah, Psalms, and Job. The most important Aquinas text is his *Summa Theologica* which can be considered as the highest systemized theological achievement of the middle ages and the basis for modern Roman Catholic theology.

Aquinas' Aristotelian influence was a process brought forward by his teacher, but he was not bound to it. At one level he also adapted Platonic doctrines handed down by St. Augustine. A fundamental concept to remember is how Aquinas made a distinction between reason and faith. Here, we begin to see the separation of science and faith. This was Thomas' attempt to rationalize the two, or to allow them to co-exist as separate but equal approaches. He believed doctrines like the Trinity, Incarnation, Creation, Original Sin, and Resurrection lie outside the scope of reason but should not be considered contrary to reason. Reason can repute arguments designed to contradict Church teachings, doctrines that come to us through revelation. The saving grace of Aquinas' teachings is his understanding that the will takes precedent over the intellect. On the other hand, truths as to the existence of God and His creative power can be discovered by natural reason altogether separate from any revelation from God.

Religion is universally thought of as a matter of faith, and science is seen as a matter of reason. But are not both dealing with truth? The truth as revealed in poetry or in one of Shakespeare's plays are different from truths posited by science; for example, every action has an equal and opposite reaction. Statements of truth can be simple: the sun rises in the east and sets in the west, and the abuse of children is never an acceptable practice. Both are true, but the statement about abusing children is outside of scientific scope. However, with the mapping of the genome and the recent advancements in genetic research, science may one day unlock a gene that indicates an individual may have genetic predispositions toward abusing or any acts of violence. Thus, we must ask ourselves are reason and faith complimentary forms of knowledge? As we will see, the answer to this question is problematic—the answer is yes and no. Take child abuse as an example. The scientific concern involves an explanation of why the abuse occurred. The religious concern is directed toward care of the individual following an abusive act: both are true and yet both are different. They are often in conflict.

Historically, theology and reason/science did walk hand in hand. The philosophies of Plato and Aristotle greatly influenced Christianity which shaped a fundamental understanding on the nature of reality within a Christ-centered context. The writings of the Apostle Paul reflect some of this philosophical influence; however, his main influence was Judaism. Paul's words in general provide a message of hope, whereas, the various philosophical movements of his day tended to be cold, neutral observations about humanity with no real answers. Whether one agrees with Christianity or not, it cannot be denied that it provides alternative answers to those of science.

Anselm (c. 1033-1109) was admired for his intellectual abilities. He was both theologian and philosopher. He served as a bridge between St. Augustine and St. Aquinas, but he somewhat broke away from Augustine in his belief that faith can be defended by intellectual reasoning and by posing arguments based on scripture and other written authorities, but like Augustine, he saw in faith as the precondition of the right use of reason. God's existence is founded on logical reasoning. Anselm believed, in regards to the existence of God, that potentiality (idea or thought) precedes actuality.

Peter Abelard (c. 1070-1142) believed faith should be rigorously examined by reason and evidence in order to uncover inconsistencies and perhaps even errors. The key point is "rigorously examined." Here, reason becomes an avenue for examining true or untrue religious experiences or scriptural understanding. Reason dictates that Jesus is not an actual door to be entered.

Once again, in the writings of Aquinas, we see a continuation of or a recovery of the writings put forth by Aristotle; however, Aquinas was never fully bound to it. A fundamental concept to Aquinas' teaching is his distinction and perhaps even separation of reason and faith. Fundamental Christian doctrines—Trinity, the Incarnation, the Resurrection—are outside the scope of reason. Such doctrines, he believed, reach us through revelation which is found in scripture and church writings. On the other hand, God's existence and God's hand in the world can be observed or detected by pure natural reason set apart from revelation.

In keeping with the Aristotelian understanding of man's nature, any argument for the existence of God must begin with the facts observed from the natural world. Essence and existence are one in God. The actions of God are a reflection of God's nature; thus, we can know God through God's creative work.

Aristotle's influences are clearly seen in Aquinas' five attributes of God: 1) All things are in motion; what started that motion to begin with? Was it God? 2) There are cause-effect relationships in the world; what was the first cause? Was it God? 3) Possibilities move to necessities; all future necessities are from God. 4) The universe is ordered from greater complexity to lower complexity. God created both the simple and the complex, and 5) the universe is ordered with a set of guiding principles, and God is the source of that order. Clearly, Aquinas is using the philosophical/scientific language of his day to try and define

God, who is truly without definition and beyond all understanding. The postmodern conflict between faith and science and the question on whether they can exist in the same realm perhaps started with Aquinas.

Martin Luther (c. 1483-1546) comes along and puts forward that reason has the potential to lead people astray because reason leads to more questions. Social-philosopher Hannah Arendt will define this as a shifting fulcrum or moving Archimedean Points. Luther's contribution to the religion and reason dialogue, when combined with the growing Renaissance interest in science and scriptural examination, help set the stage for the scientific method. The Age of Reason or the Enlightenment (1600s-1700s) and its developing confidence in science led to the questioning of religious faith and doctrine. Many positive results came out of the Age of Reason, but it also dissected and compartmentalized what it meant to be human. Humanity was no longer seen as one: body, mind, and spirit. Each component of the whole suddenly became disconnected from each other. This is one reason why academics are divided into various disciplines.

Ultimately, Aquinas' attempt to use observation and natural reason, separate from divine revelation, is futile. Theologian and Christian ethicist Stanley Hauerwas believes if we could provide the kind of evidence [that Aquinas tried to put forward] of God that those who demand evidence desire then we would bring forward evidence that the God of Christian worship does not exist, given Aquinas' understanding of science and how science contributes to our happiness as creatures of God (Hauerwas, 29).

According to Hauerwas, the Medieval Ages did not necessarily get "Christianity right." A danger exists, which started during the medieval era, for Christianity to become a status quo religion, or as Hauerwas calls it, "civilizational religion." Biblical and faithful witness takes a back seat to knowing the truth about God and God's by way of taking a scientific approach to theology. This is the slippery slope in which Aquinas gently and unknowingly pushed the place of Christianity into a downward spiral. "The very attempt to tell the story of modernity as one of decline from a genuinely Christian world ironically underwrites the assumption that the story that Christianity *is* inseparable from the story of western culture" (Hauerwas, 32).

Rene Descartes (1596-1650) brought forward Cartesian Rationalism in which great stock was put into mathematical reasoning. Rationalism has a genuine interest in the world, and there is confidence in the power of reason to understand the world (Gonzales, 185). Observation, such as the scientific method, could lead to true and significant knowledge of God. For Descartes, the first truth, or the beginning place of truth, is "I think, therefore, I am" or "*cogito, ergo sum*." Focus or emphasis is on the self and not community. Community is a concern of the Church. A second truth is God does exist. God is perfect, and because of His perfection, our minds cannot comprehend it except through the limited lens of observation. Kant was a religious man and hoped his thoughts contributed to the religious discussion. He ran into problems when theological faculties of universities declared that Aristotle's system was the best for Christianity. [Again, philosophical and intellectual language is co-opted by the Church.] Descartes believed in two parts of humanity: *res cogitans* [one that thinks] and *res extense* [occupies space]—soul and body (Gonzales, 186). The problem for Descartes—the same problem for 21st century Christianity—is how does the two relate? Descartes gives three possible solutions: 1) Occasionalism or divine intervention, 2) Monism or there is only substance of body and soul (for example, apples are round and red), and 3) Pre-established harmony set by a clock maker. Descartes, perhaps like no other, addresses the 21st century Christian condition (Gonzales, 187-88).

John Locke (1632-1704) brought to the table empiricism which basically is tied to experience. He did not believe there were innate ideas buried within us that one could discover through soul searching or by looking into one's self. All knowledge comes to us by experience—both outer and inner. This is how we come to know ourselves and the functioning of our minds. True knowledge, for Locke, comes from three levels of experience: 1) our selves, 2) outer realities before us; and 3) God's existence made known in the moment (Gonzales, 189). Apart from these, there is no certain knowledge. Faith, then, is an assent to knowledge that is derived from revelation as oppose to reason. One step further, reason and judgment must be employed to determine the degree of likelihood that we are asked to believe (Gonzales, 189). Obviously, Locke would have opposed the fanaticism of those who rely solely on divine revelation which does have disastrous potential in the likes of David Koresh or Jim Jones. Also, it is very biblical to discuss revelation in the context of community because the community helps decide revelation; in addition, community brings meaning to issues of biblical interpretation, doctrinal questions, and revelation is brought to the community for discernment.

As a side note, the Deist movement of the late 17th century became known as the free thinkers who were highly influenced by Locke, but it is fair to say that Locke more than likely distanced himself from such a label. They rejected those who were atheists and those who hold narrow views of orthodoxy. True religions, according to the Deists, must be universal or natural to all people, a part of who they are, and there can be nothing—no revelations, no historical events—that separates people from their natural urges toward religion. This partially keeps in line with the Apostle Paul's understanding of the gifts of the spirit. Paul cites the speaking of tongues as a gift, but he calls it a lesser gift in favor of more universal qualities—love, compassion, teaching, and so forth. Speaking in tongues would be considered a stumbling block for humanity's natural tendencies toward God. The Deists supported five basic doctrines: 1) the existence of God, 2) the obligation to worship God, 3) the ethical requirements of such worship, 4) the need for repentance, and 5) reward and punishment (Gonzales, 190).

David Hume (1711-1776) brought optimism to the theological table with doubt over the powers of reason. Hume argued against the Empiricists who claimed that knowledge based on experience was the only truth: see it to believe it. Hume argued no one had or has ever seen or witnessed cause and effect but it happens. For example, a billiard ball arrives at location where another ball lies. Then, a noise is heard, and the first ball stops, and the second one moves. The movement of the first ball caused the movement of the second ball. The truth, for Hume, is that nothing was actually witnessed, no cause and effect. All that is seen is a series of phenomenon from the stick, to the cue ball, to the first ball, to the second ball and final movement. Our minds link it all together. The theological problem here is that God becomes the god of the gaps. God is the One who fills the space between the billiard balls (Gonzales, 192). Hume is against all knowledge that is acquired solely through experience. But what happens when there are no more gaps to fill? Is God dead at least in the hearts of humanity under that scenario of filling the gaps?

Immanuel Kant (1724-1804) and his *Critique of Pure Reason* perhaps has influenced this science-theology debate in the postmodern era the most. Kant believed intrinsic ideas do not exist, but there are in place fundamental structures of the mind, and within these structures, we organize sensory data and file it in the proper location. Such examples are time, space, causality, existence, and substance. Thus, Kant can safely say there is no such thing as truly objective knowledge, except knowledge in other realms. Pure rationality is an illusion because there is no way to prove or disprove the existence of God and/or soul that is why the realms of science and religion are to be kept separate and kept in an amiable conflict. Reason cannot know God—just as the foot cannot know what it means to grab a glass of water. This understanding directly challenged the beliefs of his rationalistic predecessors. (Gonzales, 194-95). Since God is not understood in the same way we understand the world we cannot know God by pure reason. God can be known by an inner, moral law that determines how we make our choices in life, such as return the money or keep it when the cashier makes too much change. This inner sense of moral law gives people a sense of God, and to some degree, Kant is right. Unfortunately, such an understanding makes religion a private, personal affair rather than a faith which is communal and evangelistic in nature and always seeking social justice and reconciliation.

Natural theology plays a part in this evolution of theological interpretation of the roles of science and faith. Natural theology is the opposite of revealed theology. Paul's letter to the church at Rome states, "For all the wrath of God is revealed from heaven against all ungodliness and wickedness of those who by their wickedness suppress the truth" (Romans 1:12). One arrives at truth by thought which potentially snares faith. Natural theology was rejected by the Reformers. This does not mean there is no room for intellect. God created the human mind for solving and thinking and thus reason is good. On the contrary, it can be a valuable tool for understanding God and one's existence. John Wesley has been accredited with developing a four-prong approach to matters of faith—Scripture, Reason, Tradition, and Experience. These categories represent the totality and unity of the human experience that we bring to the theological and scientific debate.

Karl Barth (1886-1968) was the premier theologian of the 20th century. Barth was no stranger to conflict. In 1933, when the Nazis infiltrated the Church, Barth joined the "Confessing Church," along with the likes of Dietrich Bonhoeffer. The "Confessing Church" was part of the resistance against Adolph Hitler and the Nazi party. The Nazis manipulated the German Church into taking a theological stance and to articulate its relevancy. Barth strived to move theology away from the postmodern, religious philosophical interpretations of God back to a Reformation understanding and the prophetic teachings of the Bible. Barth saw in the expansiveness of God the worthlessness of humanity's attempt to understand that which is not understood. The supremacy of God and the transcendent nature of God are far beyond human comprehension. Since the Fall, humans have been under the dominion of sin, their natural capacities, their reason, and their experience. God's sole revelation is in Jesus Christ and the Word of God is how He communicates. The early theological liberalism of the early 20th century saw optimistic hope which fueled the liberal theology. However, the atrocities of two world wars cast a shadow over liberal theology; thus, Barth entered the picture to bring meaning to human crisis. Barth, who according to Hauerwas was "revealed" in paradox, believed there must be a point of contact between God and humanity, a direct revelation that is intelligible. God is completely other. God is otherness. Reinhold Niebuhr, 20th century theologian, believed that the truth of Christianity lies in its confirmation of universal and timeless myths about what it means to be human and what makes Christianity available to all people (Gonzales, 361-64).

This brief but important historical and diverse timeline of theological thought is intended to show the traditions handed down to the Church, and the forces that have shaped it. The same type of timeline for science will not be presented here because science tends to build upon itself. One theory leads to another, and to another, and so forth. Science builds upon previous thought with the outcome seen in technology. Likewise, technology also builds upon itself, such as, the old dot matrix printers to laser printers or from warehouse-sized computers which put a man on the moon to the home PC or even a smart phone that seems to do everything but cook a meal. Both have more technology than that early Apollo mission. Science is pro-active—moving forward to some unobtainable level of knowledge. Religion, the Church, historically is reactive by responding to issues of the day. This response also moves it forward to some state of perfection. How well is the Church responding to the issues of this day?

Briefly, it is important to mention Albert Einstein (1879-1955) here, because he paved modernity's way for the highly theoretical scientific models of today. The further one moves from the hard sciences the greater one is drawn toward the mystery or to the spiritual realm of infinite possibilities. Einstein was sort of religious but not in a personal God or savior way. For example, he became a moral voice in the 20th century for both Zionism and international peace. Einstein is best known by the layman for his theory of relativity. Distance and time are very much dependent upon the movement of one object relative to another object. If something passes you lengthwise, for instance, it will be shorter in length than if it were at rest. Similarly, the clock will run more slowly if it moves pass you rapidly, or if we were traveling at the speed of light, time would stop. Einstein hoped to find some unifying theory that explained everything and that united theories of sub atomic particles, energy, force, and so on. It is here where the Divine enters the picture. Is God the One who unites all things? This question will be addressed in subsequent chapters.

So, what is the role of religion and faith in a scientific, technological-driven society? From here forward, an attempt will be made to answer that question.

David Wilkerson of St. John's College, University of Durham, writes that "Christians need to stand against the tide of current trend of science bashing. The birth of postmodern science came from the Christian conviction that science was a gift from God for exploring the world and in bringing healing to creation. Responsibility given to use this gift wisely—we need to recapture that sense of gift and responsibility" (Stroble, 48).

Wilkerson is correct on several points. Science is morally neutral with the potential to do great humanitarian deeds for the advancement of quality of life as well as having the potential for destruction; first, however, the so-called "bashing" of science is not happening. There is no uproar over the technology, as result of scientific research and development, which is available today. There are perhaps two or three controversial points being attacked, such as euthanasia and evolution. Basically, science has had a free ride when it comes to technology. Based on the number of people with cellular phones, home computers, the *iPod*, and so forth, people have embraced science fully with all its technological advancements. Science and technology are seen as saviors not devils, and therefore, science is embraced. Second, Wilkerson raises the issue of our God-given responsibilities to use science properly. Here, he leans toward the theological liberalism prior to the two world wars, a theology of optimism without the reality of a broken world. As long as sin [or what will often be referred to as chaos] exists in the world, responsibility is as fragile as an egg, but responsibility must be sought after but not solely by the scientific community but also by the Church offering a resounding, "No," when science oversteps its limits. Where was the scientific community when mustard gas was invented and deployed over much of Europe during World War I? Where was the German science community when in the name of scientific research, innocent Jews were used for scientific experiments? Who was responsible when African-Americans were secretly exposed to various diseases and mind-altering drugs? Where is the responsibility in the Nuclear Age? Yes, science is a gift from God, but all God's gifts must be used wisely and to the benefit of all.

In 2007, media attention focused on pop music singer Britney Spears. She had a period of drunk driving, unmannered photographs, and general rebellion toward the courts during her child custody battles. Her life was brought into the homes through the mass media and sent all over the world for all to see via the internet. All this made possible by instantaneous technology. A website appeared, at the beginning of 2008, where people could place bets on when Britney Spears was going to die as this young woman's life was spinning out of control. Was this the intention behind the creation of the web? The World Wide Web is a good thing, but it has also given rise to a new group of pedophiles who may not have acted on their impulses if it was not for the accessibility of the inter-net. All this for one's viewing pleasure on websites. Where is people's responsibility? Is this a responsible use of technology? Technology can always be abused, especially without any checks and balances.

Current biblical and theological scholarship is not making the case for religious and Church relevancy in the West. Cable television annually around the Christmas season features programming on the Star of Bethlehem. The majority of scholars debunked a great portion of the nativity narrative; according to them, there was no star; there were no Magi; and Jesus was not born in Bethlehem but rather Nazareth because he is called Jesus of Nazareth [typically, the place where one is born is tagged onto the individual]. The problem with their understanding lies in their approach. They begin with the anthropological, archeological, and historical sciences rather than an existential beginning.

The point to the birth narrative is not whether there was an actual star or comet or what ever. The important question to ask is why did the gospel writers include it in the narrative? The Christian narrative is of an existential nature. Comets in ancient times signified the death of a king or the start of a war. Perhaps, the star announced or symbolized the death of earthly kings or the death of the old way of governing, and the birth of a new kind of kingship or governing. In other words, the gospel birth narrative pronounces the beginning of a new era. The star can be a literary device announcing the death of the old world and the birth of a new world. These understandings serve humanity better than simply trying to prove or disprove the presence of a physical star. Meaning and relevance should drive biblical scholars, theologians, and ethicists not scientific facts. Ethics are one way the Church can be relevant.

Science, as a result of the bomb shell dropped by Darwin in 1859, announced to the world that the universe follows laws that directly challenge the notion of the supernatural. Miracles are now drawn in to question, and the natural world is a self-contained causal system. The natural order is at best neutral and at worst a meaningless process. Thus, there is no freedom, no meaning, and no value to existence in the world. The world simply is, and the universe does not need a God to create it; the universe is the accidental coming together of atoms after a big bang. With this in mind and in the aftermath of Darwin's revolution, theology (historically and present day) responded and still responds in two ways: Fundamentalism and Liberalism. Fundamentalism supports biblical inerrancy, without error. No compromising biblical truths can occur. Any contradictions to the Bible are not tolerated. Liberalism, on the other hand, touts that science should go unchallenged on its own terms. In other words, one can believe in evolution while maintaining faith in a creative God, or God might have used evolution as a means of creation (Cauthen, 1-3). Liberalism acknowledges two spheres of knowledge about reality—physical and the spiritual. Instead of unifying the body and the spirit or the physical with the spiritual realms, liberalism divides the two which allows it to surrender various treatises of faith to the secular world, i.e. science. When it comes to the creation account, the approaches of fundamentalism who literally believe God created the world in seven days and liberalism who believe God could use things like evolution and the Big Bang Theory to explain the world's origins are wrong because Creation is a misguided debate and distracts from the real issues facing humanity. How, why, or when the world came into being is irrelevant. The real question is what do we do now that we are here?

According to Kenneth Cauthen, the theological sphere of faith was in fact influenced by Immanuel Kant. The previous mentioned Star of Bethlehem debate is a good example of the influence Immanuel Kant had on religious thought toward science.

Kant identified two realms: fact or science and morality or religion. Theology's role is to interpret the moral and religious realms of existence and nothing else. From a Neo-Kantian point of view, then, science and religion cannot really contradict each other because they operate on totally different realms of existence; it is like comparing apples to oranges. Ultimately, Kant and others approach the roles of science and religion as two different worlds to be dealt with in two different ways. One approach focuses upon value, meaning, purpose, and freedom, and science does not contradict nor does it support religion. The same can be said of theology, according to a Kantian understanding in regards to its relationship with science. However, this is where the Kantians and neo-Kantians fail. Science does debunk or attempt to debunk religion in the name of logic or reason or scientific/technological advancement. This may not happen consciously, but in the pursuit of scientific truth, science will run into God. It is inevitable. Likewise, religion will do the same in its pursuit of moral truth; religion will run into science as well. From a neo-Kantian point of view, realistically, religion cannot call into question scientific findings because that is not a matter of faith.

It can except them and move forward to make its own truth claims that may or may not directly come into conflict with out scientific world? The problem with keeping the realms of science in religion separate is the temptation to oversimplify: science exists in one realm, religion in another, and never the two will meet. The recent intelligent design debates in public schools and communities show how the clash between physical facts and faith values due in fact occur. Quantum physics, interdeterminancy, and chaos theories are throwing a monkey wrench into a neatly wrapped package that keeps science and religion apart. These 20th to 21st century theories have imploded the 18th to 19th century understanding of nature. Dualism is replaced by approaching "different dimensions of the same advance." Science, in other words, gives us a partial picture of a much greater hole. It is not the entire truth about the whole of reality (Cauthen, 1-10). Because of the vastness of God and our human limitations, theology or religion can likewise give us a partial picture of the whole truth.

Stanley Hauerwas probably provides the greatest indictment of Kant. Under Kant's influence, Christian theologians simply surrendered the natural world to science which created a shift to the ethical for religion, a gateway to "God." American philosopher William James defined Kant to the point of saying religious experience may only tell us something about ourselves. Ethics is a key component in the 21st Century. The work of the Church is to remind science of the stature of humanity in the world. For the Church, grace and salvation play an important role in the both the physical and spiritual realms.

The Western Church is entering its *Event Horizon*, a place much darker than the Medieval Age, because the Church of the middle age was an authoritative presence [to a fault without allowing for the balancing benefits of science, which, like all things, is created by God] in the world, and for better or for worse was the most powerful entity in Europe. If the Church is pulled into its *Event Horizon* it may not be able to return from it, from the void of a black hole at least not in its current form. So, based on other physicists' challenges to Stephen Hawking's Black Hole Theory, the best one could hope for is a memorial remnant, and thus, the Church could be reconstructed from a very simple kernel of memory—a second Great Reformation.

A black hole is so dense that its gravitational field is strong enough that neither physical matter nor radiation can escape its grasp. Is the Church or religion in general, trapped in such a dark, satanic grasp? All things are trapped and sucked into the void of nothingness. The *Event Horizon* is often described as the boundary surrounding the black hole. Upon entering the boundary particles are warped and go farther and farther into the hole. Once a particle is inside the *Horizon*, going into the void means destruction, and depending on whose theory one embraces, there may or may not be anything left. Energy, matter, space, and time are drawn into the black hole's center. But can the Western Church stop the gravitational pull toward the center of nothingness, or "irrelevancy." To stop seems like it will take more than the power to split an atom. It will take the very power of God to pull the Church from its *Event Horizon*. The world's major religions stand a great chance of being pulled into that void when technology stops becoming a tool, and starts becoming the center of existence.

The Council of Bishops of the United Methodist Church back in December, 2007 announced that a major shift in the Methodist denomination is underway due to the increase of churches overseas— mainly in Third World countries. The growth is rather dramatic. "'We are entering a new phase that the church has not encountered before because of globalization," Dallas Bishop William Oden said (Arkansas Democrat-Gazette, 4B). This growth is affecting the Methodist Church in the West. For example, a Zimbabwe bishop appointed pastors and district superintendents to England because of the Zimbabwe immigrant population there. This will shape the face of the Western Methodist Church for a while; then, once technology falls into the hands of the masses of people, Third World-Methodism will look more like the Western, Christian Church.

Why is the church growing in the Third World and not in the West? The answer is a simple one: it is all about access to technology. The average person in the West has easy access to technology due to wealth. People of the Third World do not have such access, so for them, religion takes on a deeper meaning because there is nothing else to turn to other than God, especially when surrounded by poverty and a lack of voice on the international front. The internet means nothing to a marginalized people. The Third World can be a model for the West if and only if there is a proper balance of beneficial technology with social justice, reconciliation, and compassion while respecting the beliefs of indignant

The Church, without a doubt, is facing its greatest challenge in its history. This challenge does not come from Islamic militants or some perceived immoral threat or some moral decay within society as perceived by many. However, one could argue that the West has become morally advanced in comparison to previous generations. For example, we now have laws protecting people with disabilities. Of course, humanity has a long way to go as long as wars, tyrants, and torturers live. So, the greatest challenge is how the Church remains or becomes "relevant" in a scientific, theologically-driven society where these advancements seem to provide the answers to the meaning of life like no other time before in human history.

Pope John Paul was aware of this issue. On November 15, 1980, he said our culture is a different world with science proceeding in such a way that centers on function [such as the cellular phone]. This cannot easily be applied to the cultural arena of values and norms and of spiritual matters in general. It comes down to cultural and social "relevancy." Technology and science are fulfilling that need for relevancy in people's lives for better or worse. The danger lies when technology is more than a tool. People while talking on their cell phones share personal conversation in the middle of a department store. Technology is robbing us of a fundamental right to privacy, and yet, this theft goes unnoticed and unchallenged by the Church and by humanity. Society's imbalance can be seen in the public schools. Due to budget cuts and the place of science in society, a greater emphasis is placed on mathematics and science, and a de-emphasis placed on art, music, and literature, and the complete removal of philosophy and religion. Children are going through a kind of catechesis preparing them for a technological future. Will there be another William Shakespeare, Emily Dickinson, or Sebastian Bach?

Pope John Paul believes, when science and technology enter the arena of values and norms, science runs into its own limits. When science fails [science is not perfect because people are imperfect] it creates its own crisis spilling over into society through the infiltration of technology by the consumer. The crisis is the justification of itself and purpose, "a crisis of orientation of our whole scientific culture."

Science is not able to give a complete answer to the question of the meaning of life. The question is raised in its own created crisis (Pope John Paul, 1980). The Church's crisis is simply one of finding its place in a rapidly-growing scientific culture.

The Church is nearing its *Event Horizon* being pulled into the void of irrelevancy and insignificance and nothingness—its meaning is disappearing. As long as technology remains at the center of people's lives (the genie is out of the bottle and there is no putting it back nor should it be put back because science and technology does make people's lives better), the Church must find its place in such a world; it must find its relevancy to counter-balance the influence and effect technology has on society. In the early 1970s a rather obscure movie came out titled, *Silent Running*. The movie was set in the future when humanity was venturing far into space. On earth, science and technology had destroyed the natural world on earth. Giant biospheres were built in deep space to house the remnant of creation. These spheres contained various ecosystems—northern forests, deserts, and so forth. People lived on these spheres maintaining the ships and caring for the ecosystems. A division grew between the one caregiver and those responsible for the operation and maintenance of the space ship; they ended up killing each other. By the end of the movie, the authorities on earth deemed the biosphere project too expensive, and ordered their destruction. The caregiver violated their wishes and sent one of the biospheres out into space to be cared for by a robot, and the caregiver in return, committed suicide. When humanity is separated from one another and no longer lives in community, and when people are separated from the created world, the Church, religions, and humanity cease to exist.

Chapter 2: Humanity and Science

"…with the maddening invulnerability of the stupid, looking down at the flailing hand and contorted face of the smaller boy without even a smile of satisfaction, a true scientist, observing without passion the effect of his experiment" (Rabbit, Run, 142).

Before continuing with this discussion on the role of religion in a scientific-technological society, it is important to first examine science's impact on society from a humanistic perspective. The Church is not the only one running the risk of becoming irrelevant by the rapid rise of science and technology. Humanity stands the risk of being lost in this scientific age. A portion of this book will concentrate on *humanitas* because it is here where the conflict is felt but not always recognized, and it is here where the Church will have to find itself and save humanity. There is no better documenter of science's impact on humanity than the author John Updike, especially in his four Rabbit novels that span roughly thirty years as well as some of his more recent writings.

Updike documents the beginning of the postmodern, technological age, and traces its development until its near conclusion. He raises the question: Is this good? Updike has a church background, and seems to have a fascination with science and religion as well which makes his observations an essential part of the conversation related to the role of science and technology in the world. Updike, as a fiction writer and essayist, chronicles postmodern America not from an academic perspective, but rather, from the viewpoint of middle-class America, especially through his Rabbit novels. Rabbit is the main character in four novels spanning thirty years of American, postmodern history. Segments of the Rabbit novels used in this chapter are of a sexually explicit nature. They are important because these passages describe a crucial point made in the book concerning the stature of humanity. An article in the *Christian Century* says this about Updike, "Updike was a Christian and a churchgoer. This biographical fact meant a great deal to certain Christians in search of high-brow endorsement. It might have been an embarrassment to conservative Christians who judged the sometimes sexually explicit content of his work to be vulgar or immoral. The urgent awkwardness of sexual activity was to Updike a fascinating feature of creation" (Johnson, 12). Updike is interested and concerned with humanity. The Church must not shy away from human sexuality because it is a part of what it means to be human, but take the subject head on because it has become embedded into culture.

Since the Industrial Revolution, artists, theologians, philosophers, sociologists, and so on have leveled criticisms directed toward the dehumanizing of humanity in the postmodern world due much in part to the technological advancements of the day. Writers such as the American Agrarian movement of the early 20th century and Franz Kafka and Jean-Paul Sartre lashed out against technology, such as mass production, for separating the human from humanity. This leaves humanity feeling isolated and devoid of meaning. Theologian Jurgen Moltmann in his book *Jesus Christ for Today's World* addresses the issue of "Christ After Chernobyl" in which he believes the postmodern era [even though he does not include technology but his discussion is within the framework of nuclear science] is responsible for an anthropocentric Christology (Moltmann, 88). This form of Christology, without intending to do so, gave rise to the "post-modern reduction of salvation to the salvation of the soul ..." (Moltmann, 88). This Christology may be a result of technology's ability to isolate people. Christians no longer have a concern for otherness; all that matters is the reduction of salvation to the salvation of the individual's soul with no sense of a cosmic redemption. This has disastrous repercussions, "The post-modern era has given birth to the age of ecological catastrophes. A new cosmic Christology must end the historical Christology of post-modern times" (Moltmann, 89).

From a secular perspective, Hannah Arendt, mid-twentieth century German scholar and political philosopher, gives one possible explanation for humanity's isolation and separation in her essay, "The Conquest of Space and the Stature of Man," written in 1954. This is an important essay for understanding the postmodern dilemma. Even though it pre-dates the moon launch, in prophetic fashion it addresses the issue or question of whether or not science should proceed ahead into unknown territory without regard to the dangers simply because it can while ignoring the human condition. For example, this issue is raised by the actor Jeff Goldblum in the movie *Jurassic Park*. The premise of the movie involves the discovery of genetic material from dinosaurs. Scientists, then, reproduce a variety of dinosaurs and place them on an island in order to make a dinosaur theme park. The Goldblum character makes the following point [paraphrase]: the wrong questions are being asked. It is not whether we can do this; it is whether we should be doing this. He states, "Dinosaurs and people were never meant to live together." The Church is the one institution poised to tell science, "You have gone too far."

Arendt, like many others before her, believes the advancement of science established a dichotomy in the 20th Century, creating a confrontation between the humanist and the scientist. Here, a third component may be added to this dichotomy, and that is the place of the theologian. Thus, society is caught in the middle of a triangle and pulled in three different directions, leading to the furthering estrangement of people from one another. Science has become the dominant voice in society; however, society benefits the most when humanism, science, and religion are held together in a healthy tension. Society benefits when the three are in conflict and are able to find some common ground that leads to a better world. Conflict inspires creativity. However, the conflict must be an amiable one, because hostility often stifles positive creativity, and this conflict must be on equal footing.

Arendt's pre-lunar exploration essay uses the prospect of space exploration as the medium in which this confrontation is debated. Similarly, John Updike addresses this division but within the theological and humanistic dimensions found in his four Rabbit novels: *Rabbit, Run, Rabbit Redux, Rabbit Is Rich*, and *Rabbit At Rest*. The novels illustrate the postmodern confrontation among humanists, scientists, and theologians concerning the stature of humanity. Updike's Rabbit series provides the best medium in which to study this division.

The division is best understood in terms of how each defines what it means to be human. The scientist sees humanity as mere organic creatures to be observed and conclusions drawn. Science is not interested in the importance of community for offering support to be people. This is not to say that science does not benefit humanity. Over the years, people have seen vast improvements in their quality of life, but again, science should not be the only, unchecked voice in the human narrative. The humanist promotes an attitude which lifts up or stresses the importance of human interests as opposed to the spiritual and the organic. And finally, the theologian places humanity in a cosmic/ spiritual context—whether saint or sinner or some combination of both. Basically, there is some relationship between Creator and creature or an unknowable otherness whose hand is involved in human affairs.

Thus, when considering the stature or place of individuals in the cosmic order of things either as a biological organism or as central beings subject to some higher order, a difference emerges between the concerns of the humanist and those of the scientist.

The concept or notion that there is a higher being, a set of higher ideals, or some sort of greater, unseen ordering to the universe is alien to science with some exceptions. Postmodern science has been able to emancipate itself from human concerns. For instance, take the issue of cloning. Before any attempt to clone cells begins, a fundamental question must be asked: Should we clone? Unfortunately, medical science races ahead of itself by the notion of "can we do it" rather than "should we do it." Should dinosaurs occupy the same space and time with humans? This racing ahead while failing to address the "should-we" question is dangerous because the scientist is in danger of assuming an Archimedean or scientific point of view, an understanding which overlooks the interests of the creature in the cosmos and its place in the universe. The concept of an Archimedean point of view is derived from the Greek mathematician Archimedes (287?-212 BCE). He discovered and formulated many principals of physics, but the one of importance here is the lever. He is famous for saying, "give me a place to stand, and I shall move the world" [my words]. When applied to social principals, it means humanity is searching for a place to metaphorically move their social world.

The scientist is always seeking a point of reference to measure the natural world in order to more accurately study phenomena, but as Werner Heisenberg's Uncertainty Principle points out there are limitations and inaccuracies to all human endeavors. The uncertainty principle, according to Heisenberg, "asserts that there are certain pairs of quantities, like the position and velocity of a particle, that are related in such a way that determining one of them with increased precision necessarily entails determining the other one with reduced precision" (Arendt 276). The Uncertainty Principle indicates that at the most basic level of physicality humanity lacks any ability to fully understand and to quantify any given condition of a system. Any attempt to make long-term predictions is futile when confronting nonlinear systems. The Heisenberg Uncertainty Principle as well as Chaos Theory brought an end to any notion that the universe is entirely deterministic. The Uncertainty Principle makes it clear that a prediction about future events cannot be made because we cannot even accurately measure present states. Heisenberg introduced unpredictability and randomness to a deterministic world. What does this mean? Postmodern science's attempt to find the ultimate truth will then force it into losing his objectivity of the world because the scientist will constantly search for more precise ways of measuring phenomena. Increase precision for one means a decrease in precision for another; therefore, an endless cycle of finding new measurement points, what one may call Archimedean points, is underway. Finding the ultimate point—that point from which all things or events can be precisely measured—is an illusion because science will quickly learn that the new perspective is still inaccurate. In terms of this Archimedean progression, the attempt to conquer space means that humanity through its technology will be able to journey to the Archimedean point which is anticipated by sheer force of abstraction and imagination. However, in doing so, humanity will simply diminish itself. Likewise, science continually searches for the ultimate Archimedean point on which all things hinge. This eventually diminishes humanity because it endlessly moves from one point to another trying to the answer to all of life's questions (Arendt 278). This is what drives science.

Metaphorically, the concept of an Archimedean point is modernity and postmodernist's attempt to unhinge its world and move it forward. Once society, spearheaded by science, finds a point or fulcrum for his metaphorical lever, it will soon learn that his new point is insufficient and will search for another point, and so *ad infinitum*. Cellular phones can no longer simply receive and make telephone calls. It must download music, check email, search the World Wide Web, and so forth. Each year a new application is added forcing people into a cycle of spending. This makes cellular phones no longer tools but rather task masters.

The Archimedean point concept, in conjunction with the Uncertainty Principle, also can be applied by theologians. God is the ultimate Archimedean point. This fact frees science from having to continually take into account other ethical considerations because these concerns would have already been addressed before moving forward. This can only be done if science acknowledges that there is an ultimate Archimedean point that is beyond human scope or imagination.

Harry "Rabbit" Angstrom, in John Updike's Rabbit series is the literary figure *"Everyman."* Rabbit reveals the kind of person the Church is now faced with evangelizing. The novels describe how science is having a negative impact upon humanity. Updike does this by tracing the development of his main character, Rabbit Angstrom, over four decades. In the first novel, *Rabbit, Run*, Rabbit who represents all of postmodern humanity caught up in an ever-changing world, is confused about his identity. Likewise, humanity is also confused about its identity or place in this world. Rabbit's questions are humanity's questions: Should he fully embrace this scientific and technological world and run the risk of disappearing into an ocean of knowledge? Or, should he hold on to that which makes him special in the universe? Midway through the first novel, Rabbit yields to his uncaring, cold "scientific" impulse, but by the last novel, *Rabbit At Rest,* he abandons his "scientific" inclinations—after experiencing several crises in his life. These crises chase Rabbit into a void or emptiness. Eventually, though, from out of this darkness he finds himself—his creaturely, human center. He eventually rediscovers his humanity by the final book in the series, *Rabbit At Rest*. He finds peace. The four novels are replete with many symbols or allusions to the scientists' shifting fulcrum, the void of outer space, and the issue of what it means to be human in a technological age. This is the environment in which the Church finds itself.

In the first two novels, for example, Harry Angstrom possesses the characteristics of the metaphorical scientist insofar as using Archimedes' "lever" to move or alter the course of his world. But by *Rabbit At Rest*, Harry has discovered he is lost and explores the depths of his own heart and becomes concerned with the existence of all humankind. I will be referring to Harry Angstrom's ["Rabbit"] scientific impulse throughout most of this chapter. This is not intended to be literal, but rather a way of symbolizing science/technology's influence upon society, and perhaps, the driving out of the human side and spirit side in all of us.

According to literary scholar Dean Doner, the constant descriptions throughout John Updike's *Rabbit, Run* novel of the protagonist Harry "Rabbit" Angstrom's running or moving to some unknown point, and to another unknown point, and of Rabbit's feelings of confusion and "claustrophobia," serve as a "humanistic net" thrown over Rabbit and suffocating him (Doner 18). Indeed, Updike's first Rabbit novel is replete with symbols and allusions to Rabbit's running, moving, and conquering space that may depict feelings of flight due to suffocation and unrest brought on by his uncertainty. Donor believes Rabbit needs to push beyond his existence. Instead, one can argue, the allusions of movement signify the dialectic between the humanist and the scientist in the postmodern, technological driven world. Rabbit is confused and vacillates between science and humanism impulses because the debate is argued within his heart.

Rabbit, Run uses various symbols to depict the dichotomy between the scientists' shifting fulcrum and the humanists' concern with the stature of humanity. Harry Angstrom simultaneously takes on the characteristics of the scientist and the humanist. Like the scientist, Rabbit uses Archimedes' lever to move or advance his world forward.

This allusion of being able to unhinge his world believing he can somehow control his life is best illustrated by his constant movement from relationship to relationship and his desire to move south. Moving south provides a new point where he can place his fulcrum in order to change or "move" or to control his world. Control is an illusion. Rabbit is conflicted which symbolizes the conflicted nature of society that is increasingly divided by technology. Children with access to computers and the World Wide Web have a distinct advantage over those who do not. Like the humanist, at least early in the novel, Rabbit is first concerned with matters of the heart: emotions and his own stature in the universe. We, like Rabbit, want to know who we are in the world, and are willing to take the risk by pushing beyond our own humanity in order to try to discover our humanity. Unfortunately, the end game is emptiness. Moreover, the allusion to conquering space and man's position in the world reaffirm Updike's commitment to examining humanity in the postmodern world by discussing the role of the scientist and the humanist in society. There is no better postmodern historian than Updike for tracing society's development in a new world where any and all information is just a mouse click away.

An examination of the novel could begin with a study of Rabbit's surname, which illustrates the debate or dual nature (similar to doppelganger) of Rabbit: Angst, simply put, means anxiety or remorse, a traditionally humanistic notion, and Angstrom is the scientific word meaning the unit for measuring wavelengths. Updike immediately introduces Rabbit to the reader and quickly sets up the dichotomy between the scientist and humanist via Rabbit's last name.

This dichotomy is also expressed by Updike in the third novel, *Rabbit Is Rich,* "Rabbit sees the phenomenon as he would something else in Nature—a Japanese beetle on a leaf, or two limbs of a tree rubbing together in the wind. Then he remembers, descending into the molecules, what loves feels like, huge, skin on skin, planets impinging" (*Rabbit Is Rich,* 94). The dichotomy is between feeling and observation.

Rabbit, Run can be divided into roughly three sections. The first section introduces the humanistic and scientific dichotomy existing in the postmodern, scientific age. The uncertainty which Rabbit feels because of this dual nature found in all children of modernity. The struggles of all of us in the postmodern world are symbolically debated in Rabbit's heart who truly is "Everyone." In the second part, Rabbit is clearly a humanist. By the last section of the novel, however, Rabbit has abandoned his humanistic urge in favor of his scientific impulses; this scientific impetus is carried out through the next two novels. The three sections are bound by Updike's repeated direct references to space and movement within space.

Updike introduces components of the struggle in the postmodern world early in the novel. After returning from work where he sells food processing appliances (devices to eliminate the need for knife and chopping block), Rabbit stops and plays street basketball with a group of children, trying to recapture his high school basketball glory days. After the game, he returns to his wife Janice Springer, who earlier left their son Nelson and their car at her mother's home, and by the time Rabbit arrives, she is in a drunken stupor in front of the television; thus, the reader is introduced to the dangers of the technological age. The technology of the television comforts her, but it also stupefies her. Rabbit joins his wife in watching the Mouseketeer Club. Jimmy the Mouseketeer says, "God wants some of us to become scientists some of us to become artists, some of us firemen and doctors and trapeze artists" (*Rabbit, Run,* 15).

Here one sees Rabbit suddenly becoming aware of the scientific-humanistic conflict in his world. Postmodern men and women, by Updike's use of the word, "or," in the above quote seem to be forced to choose—science or humanity. As evident today, in an age of budget cuts and prioritizing, science appears to be winning out as schools emphasize science and mathematics while cutting the arts which undercuts the human story. Men or women can be scientists or doctors; likewise, he or she can either be an artist or a trapeze performer. However, society says one cannot be both, and in a technology-based world the scientist is fast becoming the preferred choice. Jimmy the Mouseketeer finishes his discussion by saying, "So: Know Thyself. Learn to understand your talents, and then work to develop them" (*Rabbit, Run* 15). Jimmy's concluding words of wisdom seem to contradict his previous statements; however, he does pose a challenge to postmodernist mindset. That is, one must search the heart for personal truth; find a path; and follow it. Such wisdom sends mixed messages, so Rabbit is lost, and he is confused.

Rabbit is unhappy with his marriage and his job, and Jimmy's words place added pressure on Rabbit to find his place in the universe. The postmodern world relies heavily on technology; and thus, technology becomes a means to salvation. Harry Angstrom's nickname, "Rabbit," suggests that he is of the earth, of nature. Being of the earth comes into direct conflict with the synthetic world of technology. Here lies the Judeo-Christian dilemma: How can people be creaturely, children created by God, in a synthetic, technologically-driven society/culture? The Church must show them the way by helping people find their truths.

After the television episode, Janice asks Rabbit to pick up Nelson and get her a pack of cigarettes. He goes to the Springer residence and watches Nelson through a window sitting at the dinner table in a normal family situation, an environment not found in his own life. He turns and walks away, and at that moment, a stricken and confused Rabbit wants to run. He decides to leave his family and to drive south. During his drive, he reflects upon his basketball days—a time when he was sure about himself, but now, he is uncertain. While playing basketball, he followed his instincts [a non-technological characteristic], making him a good player. The postmodern world has changed him. He no longer trusts his instincts because he receives mixed messages from the world in which he lives. His uncertainty is apparent in his inability to know which roads to take to reach the South. This uncertainty and failing instincts place Rabbit in a state of despair. Rabbit's vision of himself is telling, "He [Rabbit] images himself about to shoot a long one-hander; but he feels he's on a cliff, there is an abyss [i.e. Hawking's black hole/void] he will fall into when   the ball leaves his hands" (*Rabbit, Run*, 28). The ball has now left his hands, and he is lost. Rabbit is searching for position; that is why he is going south. He wants to find a new "point" in order to change his situation. He needs a fulcrum and a place to stand to unhinge his current reality.

When Rabbit pulls off the road to fuel his car and purchase a map, a scientist, in the guise of a gas attendant, tells Rabbit, "The only way to get somewhere is to decide where you're going and go" (*Rabbit, Run* 37). In other words, one should form a hypothesis and test it. The gas attendant, to whom Rabbit refers as a "scholar," is teaching the student Rabbit. Finally, Rabbit's confusion is evident when he quickly darts off the road shortly after leaving the attendant to study his map, "There are so many red lines and blue lines, long names, little towns, squares and circles and stars" (*Rabbit, Run*, 39). Again, Rabbit, like humanity, receives mixed messages in regards to our existence. In a frustrated state brought on by his lack of direction in life, Harry ends up tearing his map into pieces and frantically driving off. Anxiously, "He claws at it and tears it; with a grasp of exasperation he rips[the utter destruction found in Hawking's black hole where matter is torn apart to the sub-atomic level and beyond] away a great triangular piece and tears the large remnant in half and, more calmly, lays these three pieces on the top of each other and tears them in half, and then those six pieces and so on until he has a wad he can squeeze in his hand like a ball" (*Rabbit, Run* 39). Rabbit's agony is strongly felt here. The culmination of a lack of direction, a failing marriage, meaningless and worthless employment, and an unconscious struggle in a technological world weigh heavy on Harry's heart. What is the point of it all?

After Rabbit's bout of confusion, he aborts his efforts to flee to the south and returns to his hometown, Brewer. Instead of going to his apartment, he runs to his basketball coach, Coach Tothero. One critic believes Rabbit goes to his old high school coach's apartment because Tothero is the only person who let him run, to simply "be." (Doner, 26). People desire freedom, and technology imprisons people by driving them to consume more and more of it, to spend more and more, to upgrade more and more. Rabbit's coach provides additional allusions to the dichotomy or the two opposing views prevailing in the postmodern world: science or humanity [includes religion]. Rabbit asks Tothero about how to help his marriage and Janice's drinking problem, and Tothero responds by saying, "'Perhaps you should have,' Tothero offers after a moment. 'Perhaps if you had shared this pleasure [drinking] with her, she could have controlled it'" (*Rabbit, Run*, 45). Whether misplaced or twisted, the nature of his answer to Rabbit's question is clear: healing and reconciliation comes out of relationship, human-to-human contact, albeit Tothero puts forward a highly questionable approach. Again, a world without science is frightening because it plays an important role in improving the quality of life. Science cannot be the only agent of healing and reconciliation. Shortly after Rabbit's discussion with his coach, Tothero offers an even more humanistic response to Rabbit. Rabbit questions Tothero, "He [Rabbit] says sharply, 'So you think I should've drunk with Janice.'" "'Do what the heart commands,' Tothero says. 'The heart is our only guide'" (*Rabbit, Run,* 53). People are hungry for meaning, and are searching for guidance.

The basketball coach offers Harry a new option, a new fulcrum; he introduces Rabbit to Ruth, a prostitute. Rabbit's failing marriage and uncertain life force him to move to a new point, i.e. Ruth's apartment, to try to change his world and to end his confusion. In other words, if one hypothesis fails, one should try another one from a different perspective. One moves from one hypothesis to another only to find the ultimate truth to be elusive. Here Rabbit begins to examine his scientific impulse that has now become part of human nature in this postmodern age, but he is not quite ready for the scientific way of life. Moreover, once a scientist has tried a hypothesis, he is driven to keep testing hypotheses, to go one step further [this is clearly illustrated by the end of the novel]. Scientific knowledge builds upon past accomplishments and studies. Rabbit's original Archimedean point or fulcrum was high school basketball. After high school, Harry immediately married Janice Springer, i.e. his new Archimedean point. When the Janice experience had been tested and reached to a conclusion, he moves on to a new fulcrum or Archimedean Point, i.e. Ruth's bedroom. The confusion Rabbit feels is brought on by his constantly shifting fulcrum, his uncertainty, his constant need to move from point to point.

After Rabbit's affair with Ruth, he is introduced to Rev. Eccles, who works to bring Rabbit and Janice back together. This episode is laden with references to the humanist/scientist debate. Eccles and his wife Lucy illustrate the debate: Eccles ironically represents the humanist and not the theologian, and Lucy symbolizes the scientist. Eccles is concerned with the daily affairs of people. He wants to get involved, as indicated by his many attempts to bring Harry and Janice back together. His humanistic concerns put him at odds with the scientific world.

His wife Lucy, on the other hand, takes a Freudian, scientific approach to life. With several of Sigmund Freud's books on the shelf, the minister's wife constantly reflects upon a Freudian psychoanalytical approach toward her husband Eccles and to her children. For example,

Lucy tells Rabbit, "Children are very sacred in psychology" (*Rabbit, Run,* 119). We can infer that children have been reduced to an object to be observed. The different approaches create a conflict within the Eccles' household, pitting husband against wife and mother against daughter. The Eccles' household is a microcosm of what is happening in the postmodern world and within Rabbit's confused heart—the needs of humanity in conflict with a technological-driven world.

All of Rabbit's confusion and uncertainty about his life, existence, and his affair with Ruth force him to examine his own stature or position in the universe. Rabbit thinks, "It seems plain, standing here, that if there is this floor there is a ceiling, that the true space in which we live is upward space. Someone is dying. In this great stretch of brick someone is dying. The thought comes from nowhere: simple percentages" (*Rabbit, Run* 108). Rabbit ponders this question while he is in bed with Ruth. Thinking about his own stature frightens him, and he begs Ruth, "Put your arm around me" (*Rabbit, Run* 108). He needs human comfort in a cold, scientific age of synthetics and microchips. The Church is called to be those arms wrapped around humanity. Updike employs a precise metaphor to describe the stature or position of humanity in the universe. Simply, there is the earth and the sky, and humans are somewhere in between. The scientist does not care about humanity's stature. Humanity's stature in the universe is the concern of humanists and theologians. Rabbit's thoughts about his place in the world sum up the nature of the first Rabbit novel dealing with the stature and position of humanity in the universe.

During his basketball days, Harry Angstrom never thought much about his existence. Suddenly, he is an adult thrust into the postmodern world that sends him mixed messages. The narrator says, "That was the thing about him [Rabbit], he just lived in his skin and didn't give a thought to the consequences of anything" (*Rabbit, Run* 139). Here, Updike emphasizes Rabbit's sudden awareness of the postmodern, external world and his place in it. Rabbit can no longer hide behind the basketball days of youth.

Most of the novel presents Rabbit's confusion, and Updike uses this confusion as a symbolic battleground between science and humanism. Shortly after Rabbit's awareness of the question surrounding humanity's stature, Updike warns the reader of what Arendt believed was the final consequence of science, the existential destruction of humanity when humanity encounters that void or vacuum in the universe. He writes, "…the whole frame of blood and bone must burst in a universe that can be such a vacuum" (*Rabbit, Run* 142). This is an accurate description of a Black Hole. The description of the void of a Black Hole occurs when Eccles tries to bring Rabbit and Janice back together. While working with Rabbit and Janice, Eccles also is observing Rabbit's son Nelson and his friend Billy Fosnacht playing together. Updike offers a warning about the dangers of acting solely on our scientific impulse without proper checks and balances. Eccles also sees the danger by briefly exchanging his humanistic hat for that of the scientist. He is watching the children—Nelson and Billy Fosnacht—fight with detached observation and without regard for potential injury. Billy is beating up Nelson. Eccles does not seem to care, and Updike ironically likens The Rev. Eccles to a scientist, "Young Fosnacht stands fast, with the maddening invulnerability of the stupid, looking down at the flailing hand and contorted face of the smaller boy without even a smile of satisfaction, *a true scientist, observing without passion the effect of his experiment*" [emphasis mine] (*Rabbit, Run,* 142). Eccles, with "twisting heart," realizes how easy it is to be the "true scientist," the neutral observer, and falls into that void or "vacuum." This is humanity's *Event Horizon*, the desire for knowledge beyond human understanding—knowledge reserved for God—led to the Fall in the Garden of Eden.

The science verses humanity confrontation presents itself to the reader not only through the characters; it is also delivered through Updike's poetic description. He writes, "Warmth vibrates in brown and purple arcs between the lights of the service station and the moon" (*Rabbit, Run,* 35), and "A damp warm cloth seems wrapped around his (Rabbit's) heart" (*Rabbit, Run,* 182). Conversely, Updike's narrative style also communicates this dichotomy between science and humanity. Updike can be as scientifically precise and mathematical with his narration as he is poetic; for example, Updike uses precise mathematical language when describing Rabbit's destruction of the map at the beginning of the novel. Another of Updike's mathematical narrations is found in a brief description of Rabbit's home city of Brewer, "Club Castanet was named during the war when the South American craze was on and occupies a triangular building where Warren

Avenue crosses Running Horse Street at an acute angle" (*Rabbit, Run*, 160). Here, Updike uses geometry to describe a location, and he uses geometry and basic mathematics to describe Rabbit's destruction of his map when he tears it into triangles.

The difficulty faced by postmodern society lies in reconciling science, humanism, and theology in a cultural and societal reality dominated by the presence of science and technology. Arendt believes there is a difference between the concerns of the scientist and those of the humanist (Arendt 265). According to Arendt, the idea that man is the highest being is foreign to the scientist, and the "glory" of postmodern science is to separate itself from humanistic concerns (Arendt 265-66). This philosophic notion is related in a passage midway through *Rabbit, Run*. Updike writes, "He [Eccles the humanist] seems unreal to Rabbit, everything seems unreal that is outside of his sensations" (*Rabbit, Run* 183). This peek into Rabbit's mind appears to define the role of the scientist. Scientists study only observable, physical phenomena or physical "sensations," such as smell, taste, sight and touch. Updike also presents the distance between the scientist and humanist, "He [Rabbit] must know the facts yet seems unaware for the gap of guilt between Harry and humanity" (*Rabbit, Run*, 187).

As one can see, most of *Rabbit, Run* describes the dichotomy in the postmodern world through Rabbit's confusion and internal struggles. In this first novel, Rabbit has not fully embraced the technological, postmodern world; he struggles with the remnant of humanism still within him that resists the cold, neutrality of science. Pressure mounts, however, for him to abandon those humanistic qualities in favor of a detached, world view.

The humanistic quality of Rabbit compared to his "scientific" disposition is expressed only a few times. Doner believes Rabbit's humanism is a negative quality, "He (Rabbit) is not a spokesman for, but like all other characters in the book, a product of Western Humanism" (Doner 23). On the contrary, the humanistic side of Harry Angstrom is his saving grace; this is made clear by the last Rabbit book *Rabbit At Rest*.

Harry Angstrom is concerned with the results of his actions, such as leaving his wife and living with Ruth. He wonders if his son Nelson's psyche will be damaged by all his moving around. He also worries about Janice, and his concern leads him to reflect upon his entire life. Rabbit's best days have been during his high school basketball career, which occurred before the Atomic Revolution [Arendt designates the development of the Atomic Bomb as the dividing point between the old and postmodern world]. Harry Angstrom describes the best part of his life in existential terms by reminiscing about his playground and basketball days. He also elevates and fantasizes about his individual accomplishments on the court. Those days are gone and Rabbit finds himself struggling.

Several other references to the anxiety happening within Rabbit's heart appear. Keep in mind Updike uses the ancient understanding of the human heart—the heart is the place of one's character, moral center, essence, and being. References can be found directly describing Harry's heart, "The artificial sweetness fills his heart" (*Rabbit, Run* 208). The "artificial sweetness" describes the synthetic world in which humanity finds itself. Rabbit's past, present and future weigh heavy on his heart throughout his brief humanistic period in the novel. The narrator says, "And meanwhile his heart completes its turn and turns again, a wider turn in a thinning medium to which the outer world bears a decreasing relevance" (*Rabbit, Run,* 269). Updike's use of the metaphor, "his heart completes its turn," indicates some sort of struggle or conflict within Rabbit's heart, a clearly traditional notion of the humanist who examines the weight of human experience. The outside, postmodern world is pressing down on Harry Angstrom, and his heart is being worn thin as is all of humanity.

Wearisome comes from humanity's inability to find itself in an ever-changing world shaped and re-shaped by technology. Science shows that there is an infinite universe out there which raises questions never asked before in history and many of those questions have yet to be answered. Yet, more and more people turn to science for their answers rather than the Church. We are at a three-way intersection where science, religion, and humanism come together. Rabbit's humanistic and his scientific impulses overlap, but there is a distinct point in the novel in which Rabbit abandons his humanistic side. This drives him toward the cold, silence of the universe. Harry Angstrom abdicates his humanity when he runs off from the burial of his newborn daughter, who was accidentally drowned when Janice was intoxicated. Science cannot address the issue of life and death in such a way that brings comfort to those who grieve. Doner believes Rabbit's running from the burial indicates that "the real shock is Updike's illumination of the true nature of Humanism" (Doner 32). However, Doner fails to see that after the estranged Rabbit comes back to Janice the first time. While she is still in the hospital with their new baby, Harry Angstrom's humanity is not entirely gone. But after he leaves Janice the second time, which results in Janice's drunkenness and subsequently the drowning of her, Rabbit becomes more distant from humanity. In scientific fashion, he is an observer not a participant.

Midway into the novel Rabbit's mother makes a brief allusion to her son's metaphorical, Archimedean scientific impulse. His mother describes Rabbit as being similar to a scientist, while she is using a "lever" in the kitchen to release ice cubes, Updike writes, "'When he [Rabbit] set his mind to something,' Mrs. Angstrom says [to Eccles], 'there was no stopping him.' She yanks powerfully at the lever of the ice-cube tray and with a brilliant multiple crunch that sends chips sparkling the cubes come loose" (*Rabbit, Run*, 152). Updike associates Rabbit with the lever. Rabbit, like the scientist, "sets his mind to something" and goes out and tests it. Rabbit applies leverage to accomplish what he wants. It is that "leverage" that may push humanity to the edge of space, to the edge of what it means to be human.

As noted earlier, Rabbit drops his humanistic impulse during the burial of his daughter. When Rabbit decides to run from the burial services, he decides to leave humanity behind, according to Updike, "Once inside, he [Rabbit] is less sheltered than he expected: turning, he can see through the leaves back down the graveyard to where, beside the small green tent, the human beings he had left cluster" (*Rabbit, Run*, 272). Updike clearly states that Harry Angstrom has separated himself from humanity by leaving the humans behind. Likewise, Arendt believes that scientists are not concerned with humanity from an existential point of view. They are only concerned with scientific discovery. She explains, "This view [the Roman notion of humanity as the highest beings] of man is even more alien to the scientist, to whom man is no more than a special case of organic life …" (*Rabbit, Run*, 266). Science has contributed much to the benefit of humanity, but do not forget there is another side, a side that must be kept in check. The view expressed by Arendt is the destructive element of science.

Once Harry Angstrom begins to leave humanity behind, he has one last chance to salvage his humanity. Updike goes into a long descriptive narrative elaborating Rabbit's confusion as he is running from the cemetery. Rabbit wants to return to the others, but his guilt prevents him. He keeps on walking away, "If he [Rabbit] walks far enough uphill he will in time reach the scenic drive that runs along the ridge. Only by going downhill can he be returned to the others" (*Rabbit, Run* 273).

This passage illustrates Rabbit's unconscious decision to accept the role of the scientist. [However, throughout the Rabbit series, Harry Angstrom is unable to fully let go of that last kernel of humanity.] Arendt believes scientists are driven upward or outward into space in order to change their world (Arendt, 278-79). Similarly, Rabbit is driven "uphill" to change the situation, to move it some how. He searches for a place to place his "fulcrum" in order to move his world. If he walks down the hill, Harry Angstrom will re-join humanity. The above passage is a metaphor of the scientist's desires to always move ahead and go beyond his point of origin, i.e. search for a new Archimedean point. Rabbit elects not to return "to the others;" instead, he flees to Ruth's apartment, the final scene in *Rabbit, Run*. His moving up the hill and running to Ruth's apartment reveals Rabbit's search for a new Archimedean point. Ruth is that point, but he will learn that his efforts are futile, and he will be forced to search for a new Archimedean point. The four Rabbit novels depicts Rabbit desperately searching for that Archimedean point that will change or move his world in a direction that will some how bring peace of mind. According to Heisenberg's Uncertainty Principal, that will be a difficult task. This is the plight of humanity in the postmodern world. This is where the Church must define itself.

According to Arendt, a scientist—through his constant attempts to find new Archimedean points, such as space exploration, or the constant expansion of his scientific capabilities—can only get lost in the greatness of the universe. Technology is driving us away from our humanity because no balance is being sought between the benefits, such as improved medical care, of technology and the importance of human, face-to-face interaction, just as Rabbit is driven away from his. Oddly, there is never a direct connection made between Rabbit and technology's influence; however, it is the narration that reveals an underlying current of science's sway. The only true Archimedean point would be the absolute void in the universe; this means the lowering of man's stature (Arendt, 274-76). Updike makes several allusions to this void in *Rabbit, Run*. The references to the "void" in the first novel foreshadow the void Rabbit discusses but never understands in *Rabbit Redux* and Arendt's void in the universe. He eventually understands it in *Rabbit Is Rich*.

The consequences of Rabbit's attempts to move or to change his world unfold in the last seven pages of the novel. His lover Ruth is pregnant, and Rabbit sincerely wants to marry her, but he cannot because of his marriage to Janice. Rabbit realizes his situation and concludes the only solution is to move away from his current situation, i.e. find a new Archimedean point. Updike makes a reference to a lever and sums up the situation, "Ruth and Janice both have parents: with this thought he dissolves both of them. Nelson remains: here is a hardness he must carry with him. On this *small fulcrum* [emphasis mine] he tries to balance the rest, weighing opposites against each other … (*Rabbit, Run* 282-83). Rabbit's lever reminds us of the false security provided by science. Meteorology accurately predicted the landfall of Hurricane Katrina, but there is nothing it could do about it. Science cannot motivate people to bring aid, support, and love. People motivate people. Every time meteorology makes a landfall prediction, and if the prediction is incorrect or the size of the storm diminishes before coming ashore, then, people are lulled into a false sense of disbelief, so they do not leave the area. The above fulcrum passage exhibits some interesting points about Rabbit's scientific impulse. The most obvious is the statement about the fulcrum. First, Harry Angstrom's mother recognizes his scientific impulse; now, Rabbit acknowledges his impulse. Second, Rabbit is acting as a scientist by observing his situation in life and weighing the facts to come to some conclusion. Finally, Rabbit "dissolves both of them [Ruth and Janice]." In other words, he metaphorically destroys their humanity. The Church's role is to bring it back from the edge of its Event Horizon.

Rabbit returns to his wife at the end of *Rabbit, Run*. One may argue that he is not setting a new Archimedean point; instead, he seems merely to be returning to the point from which he came. The last paragraph, however, seems to suggest otherwise, "He [Rabbit] wants to travel to the next patch of snow [i.e. next fulcrum]. Although this block of brick three-stories is just like the one he left, something in it makes him happy; the steps and window sills seem to twitch and shift in the corner of his eye, alive. This illusion trips him" (*Rabbit, Run* 284). The passage suggests he has returned to a new and different wife, i.e. world. His wife Janice, throughout the other novels, becomes more independent, taking more control of family matters and finances. In *Rabbit, Run* the old Janice is weak and takes no initiative. Indeed, Rabbit has come back to a different world. With every technological step forward, humanity moves to a different world, losing itself with each step. Different worlds are being created faster than at any point in the history of the world.

The novel can be expressed in terms of humanity's conundrum—what it means to be human in a synthesized, technological-driven world where science dominates culture and people are search for meaning. Updike's constant references to space and the universe connect the sections.

Even though *Rabbit, Run* was written before the Apollo 11 mission, Updike makes references to space travel and the attempts by the Soviet Union and the United States to be the first country to put a man in outer space. The space race was underway when the book was published. Updike writes, "Now he [Rabbit] must move. He feels unreasoning fear of being taken over" [by technology] (*Rabbit, Run,* 40). Later, Updike writes, "In the sky two perfect disks, identical in size but the one a dense white and the other slightly transparent, move toward each other slowly ..." (*Rabbit, Run,* 260). The two statements are allusions to the United States and Soviet Union's competition to put a man into space. Both times Rabbit is alone and trying to accomplish some goal. The first reference to "unreasoning fear" comes at the beginning of *Rabbit, Run* when Rabbit is trying to flee to the South, but he cannot quite get there. He turns back. The second reference appears before the funeral, when Rabbit is on the verge of awakening from a dream and abandoning his humanistic side. In this case, he is trying to overcome his guilt brought on by the death of his baby girl, but he cannot do so. The void of the universe is used as an explanation for death, "He understands: `the cowslip' is the moon, and `the elder' the sun, and that what he has witnessed is the explanation of death: lovely life eclipsed by lovely death" (*Rabbit, Run,* 260). Moreover, Updike makes references to celestial bodies, " ...the yellow center of a second moon" (*Rabbit, Run,* 71); "Wake up with the stars above perfectly spaced in perfect health" (*Rabbit, Run,* 126); and "Sun and Moon, sun and moon, time goes" (*Rabbit, Run,* 127). Science hears the call of outer space and cannot resist. Updike also gives a description of the galaxy with its arms projecting out into the universe as well as its formation, "And farther inside, so ghostly it comes to him last, hangs a jagged cloud, the star of an explosion, whose center is uncertain in refraction but whose arms fly from the core of pallor as straight as long eraser-marks diagonally into all planes of the cube" (*Rabbit, Run,* 85).

While Rabbit plays basketball, Updike makes one direct reference to science's attempt to move into space and thus the ultimate demise of humanity via conquering space resulting in humanity's disappearance into the universe. He writes, "Rabbit thinks it will die, but he's fooled, for the ball makes his the ground of a final leap: with a kind of visible sob takes a last bite of space before vanishing in falling" (*Rabbit, Run,* 126). The "last bite of space" describes the consumption of space; unfortunately, the universe's vastness prohibits it from being fully consumed, so science finds itself constantly taking small bites.

So, what is Rabbit? Doner suggests Rabbit is both "Christ-life and Satan-death." In other words, there is a doppelganger nature of Harry Angstrom. Instead of Christ-life and Satan-death, Rabbit is humanist-man and scientist-space, but by the end of the novel he is mainly the metaphorical scientist from an Arendt/Archimedean perspective. The Church is currently unclear concerning what humanity really is. When the Church defines what it means to be human, it will define itself. Again, science is not to be understood literally. Harry Angstrom's scientific nature represents the influence science has on humanity which changes how people interpret the world. Rabbit as scientist is carried over into *Rabbit Redux*, where Rabbit observes the inter-action of people and the Apollo 11 mission.

In *Rabbit Redux* the year is 1969, and Rabbit is roughly ten years older than he was in *Rabbit, Run*; no one except the narrator calls him

Rabbit. United States troops are fighting in Vietnam, and NASA is about to send Apollo 11 and its crew to the moon. The hippie counter-culture and the Civil Rights movements are moving forward; and Harry Angstrom—picking up where he left off in *Rabbit, Run*—reveal his scientific desire by observing the changing country around him. Harry has a job working as a linotype setter with his father Earl Angstrom at the local printing plant, and Janice and Harry have moved out of their apartment into a house in the Penn Villas community.

Rabbit Redux begins with a long, pessimistic narrative about the state of affairs in his town called Brewer, "Men emerge pale from the little printing plant at four sharp, ghosts for an instant, blinking, until the outdoor light overcomes the look of constant indoor light clinging to them. In winter, Pine Street at this hour is dark, darkness presses down early from the mountain that hangs above the stagnant city of Brewer" (*Rabbit Redux*, 13). The emerging men from the printing plant are significant. One of the byproducts of technological discovery was the Industrial Revolution. The dark side of the Industrial Revolution led to the de-humanizing of individuals, families, and communities. One was owned by the company store.

This opening narrative is significant in that it sets the tone of the novel. Images of death and destruction are everywhere, and Updike creates this dismal environment to criticize the scientific age, and he uses the ultimate symbol of scientific achievement—putting a man on the moon to frame his argument. Rabbit is the metaphorical "scientist" (as previously described by Arendt) who must remain neutral and objective. He no longer concerns himself with humanity; Harry's concern is to observe and to study the world around him no matter the consequences. *Rabbit Redux* portrays Rabbit as the "scientist," and Updike communicates this portrayal by tying images of space exploration, such as beginning every chapter with a quote from either American or Soviet astronauts and by using scientific descriptions in association with him. To further illustrate Harry's lost humanity and how it has been replaced with a scientific-Archimedean point of view, Updike works into the narration frequent references to synthetic products such as plastic, chemicals, and cosmetic limbs.

Updike's penchant for history and fiction is seen as he introduces humanity's greatest scientific achievement—the moon landing. Early in the novel, Harry and his father are in a bar, a daily ritual after work. The narrator says, "The bar television is running, with the sound turned off. For the twentieth time that day the rocket blasts off, the numbers pouring backwards in tenths of seconds faster than the eye until zero is reached: then the white boiling beneath the tall kettle, the lifting so slow it seems certain to tip, the swift diminishment into a retreating speck, a jiggling star" (*Rabbit Redux,* 16). Emphasis should be on "diminishment into a retreating speck" because it indicates the lessening of human stature in a technological age. Humanity is no longer the center of the universe because science moves farther and farther outward into space pulling humanity along with it until humanity's its stature is gone in the vastness of the universe. The description of the television set may seem unimportant, but its purpose is to show the significance of the lunar mission at the time. Across the country, people had their television sets tuned into this historic voyage. After Harry and his father discuss the launch, their conversation shifts to Harry's mother, who has Parkinson's Disease. Earl tells his son, "Already, you know, there aren't any more crazy people: just give'em a pill morning and evening and they're sensible as Einstein" (*Rabbit Redux,* 17). In his working class manner, Earl Angstrom is commenting on scientific advancement, and how science has entered the household; science has penetrated the home, and the amount of technology present in a home today is greater than during any other period in time. The decline of the family can possibly be connected to the introduction of more and more technology into the home. People no longer talk because of television, DVRs, DVDs, personal computers, smart phones, and whatever technological device one can imagine. There is no longer a sense of everyone contributing to the operations of the family or community.

Charles Berryman in his essay, "The Education of Harry Angstrom: Rabbit and the Moon," comments on this bar scene, especially the television description and Updike's fictional news broadcasts of the launch peppered throughout the novel. Berryman claims the characters are unable to make sense of the news; they are only interested in "soldiers and astronauts" (Berryman, 119). Berryman's insight into the characters may be true, but one can argue Rabbit is genuinely interested in the Apollo 11 mission. Harry can relate to the astronauts because

Rabbit and the Apollo 11 crew are undertaking a similar exploration [one that may have deadly consequences if not kept in check by some outside entity]. Berryman appears to draw similar conclusions, "Harry may not travel to the moon and back, but he is exploring the space inside of the heart" (*Rabbit Redux*, 122). Harry also is exploring the hearts of his wife Janice and his son Nelson. He also will invite two outsiders into his home in order to study the hearts of Jill and Skeeter, two people from the counter-culture movement. His need to study and observe makes him completely unaware of the psychological damage he is doing to his son Nelson.

After Harry leaves his father at the bar, he boards the bus for home. During his bus ride, insight into Rabbit's newly discovered scientific impulse is revealed. He is studying or examining the blacks on the bus. Rabbit thinks, "Negroes instead of being more primitive are the latest thing to evolve, the newest men." The narrator goes on to say, "being smart hasn't amounted to so much, the atom bomb and the one-piece aluminum beer can" (*Rabbit Redux*, 21). Thus, the hidden potential for science and technology as being a destructive force is revealed, therefore, a price is paid with all advancements; for example, genetic research may lead to the treatment of genetic-related disorders, but it also may be used for biological weapons.

Rabbit's first encounter with the African-Americans on the bus has been criticized. One critic, Edward Jackson, believes Rabbit is a racist because he tends to separate himself from blacks, but the bus passage is not necessarily a racial slur. Harry is acting on his "scientific" impulse to observe what is happening around him. He separates himself from the phenomenon to remain neutral. The passage is ironic in that the narrator mentions Darwin's theory of evolution, a revolutionary theory that changed the scientific community as much as or even more so than the Apollo 11 mission.

Later the same day, additional insight into Rabbit's psyche is given by the narrator. Harry and his son Nelson watch television, waiting for Janice, who is having an affair with co-worker Charlie Stavros, to return from work. Harry is upset with Nelson's lack of interest in sports. The narrator says, "That's the trouble with caring about anybody, you begin to feel overprotective. Then you begin to feel crowded" (*Rabbit Redux*, 26). This crowded feeling is the same crowded feeling described at the end of *Rabbit, Run* when Rabbit leaves the "humans" gathered at his daughter's funeral and runs up the hill. The narrator's look into Rabbit's psyche echoes Arendt's belief that scientists separate themselves from humanity. Technology can be the perfect vehicle for this separation as described by Rabbit's uncaring attitude. Rabbit is uncaring toward other human beings and chooses not to be emotionally involved. In Rabbit's mind, caring for people causes problems, so Harry separates himself from humanity by detaching himself from his emotions. There is where the danger lies. Science and technology does not connect us to our emotions nor does it form community. In fact, the age of computers and genetics isolate us. A nuclear scientist working for the Department of Defense must detach himself or herself from the nightmarish loss of lives if a nuclear weapon is deployed. The Church can play a crucial role here by reconnecting science to humanity by pointing out some consequences scientific discovery may or may not have upon people.

The narrator mirrors Arendt's point that the human race can only lose itself in the greatness of the universe if its sole scientific purpose is to go deeper and deeper into space thereby destroying humanity; this foreshadowing is evident in the gloomy descriptions of the town of Brewer, depicting a bleak and lifeless world, and Rabbit's uncaring attitude toward the people around him. Harry is more interested in exploring the depths of people: not for the sake of humanity or community but to quench his own scientific, self-centered need to know. Arendt uses the space program to illustrate her point. She believes that once humans have stepped on the moon, humanity cannot stop there; science will go beyond the moon into the emptiness of outer space. It is there where humanity is lost. The only place in space where science can finally stop is nothingness or The Event Horizon (Arendt, 265-80). Similarly, Updike writes, "The six o'clock news is all about space, all about emptiness: some bald man plays with little toys to show the docking and undocking maneuvers, and then a panel talks about the significance of this for the next five hundred years. They keep mentioning Columbus but as far as Rabbit can see it's the exact opposite: Columbus flew blind and hit something, these guys see exactly where they're aiming and it's a big round nothing" (*Rabbit Redux*, 28).

Arendt and Updike are similar in that they recognize the destructive nature of space exploration, which is the epitome of scientific, technological advancement. Arendt claims humanity will eventually find the void, the *Event Horizon*, and subsequently death. Likewise, Updike writes, "these guys see exactly where they're aiming and it's a big round nothing." In *Rabbit, Run* the narrator would not have made such observations because Harry was too busy struggling with his dual nature: humanity and science. Updike frequently uses scientific terms to illustrate Rabbit's developing scientific vocabulary, to display his protagonist's pseudo-scientific side, "He [Rabbit] was dreaming about a parabolic curve, trying to steer on it, though the thing was fighting him, like a broken sled" (*Rabbit Redux,* 32). Here, Rabbit thinks like a scientist. W.F. Hilton observed that satellites orbit the earth in patterns that resemble parabolic curves. Elliptical orbits are the most efficient because this type of orbit allows satellites to carry a larger payload. Elliptical orbits are two parabolic curves joined together (Hilton, 35-37). The reference to the parabolic curve not only demonstrates Harry's scientific vocabulary, but it also indicates how Rabbit wants to bring order into his life. The parabola is mentioned during a long narration describing Harry's falling in and out of sleep. Rabbit feels his life with Janice is spinning wildly in space, "though the thing [his life] he was trying to steer was fighting him ..." and " ...he is seeking to hold to a curving course to a nest ..." (*Rabbit, Redux,* 32). The elliptical orbit (two parabolic curves) that satellites make around the earth is controlled motion. Satellites are not spinning out of control. The parabolic curve the narrator mentions is a set, geometric path that seems to convey Rabbit's desire to get his life under control by following a set pattern. Instead of spinning through life, i.e. outer space, out of control, he is thinking of ways to put his life in orbit, i.e. ordering his universe.

Harry and Janice discuss going out to dinner at a Greek restaurant followed by seeing the movie, *2001: A Space Odyssey.* Janice complains about the movie, "'Women don't dig science'" (*Rabbit Redux,* 40). The narrator responds, "Women and nature forget. No need for science since they are what science seeks to know" (*Rabbit Redux,* 41). This insertion by the narrator is substantial because Harry is trying to understand women; he wants to study women and in order to do so he must study as many metaphorical "specimens" as possible, such as Ruth in *Rabbit, Run* and his eventual affairs with Jill and Peggy Fosnacht in *Rabbit Redux.* The more test samples he studies the better Rabbit understands himself but the further he drifts from humanity. Rabbit's need to know distances himself from the very things that fascinate him.

Rabbit and his family go to the Greek restaurant, where Updike introduces Charlie Stavros, a Greek, to the reader. Stavros sits down with them and helps the family order from the menu. Janice interrupts, "We're trying to get to see this silly space movie." Stavros says, "I guess I don't find technology that sexy" (*Rabbit Redux*, 45). A political argument over the Vietnam War breaks out between Harry and Charlie: Harry supports the war, and Charlie opposes it. Nelson and Janice side with Charlie, making Rabbit feel out of place. In this scene, Rabbit is the "scientist" among the "humanists." This division between Harry and Charlie and Janice represents the separation between the humanist and scientist. There is no sense of cooperation. This distinction between science and humanism—as expressed by Harry, Charlie, and Janice—is a healthy one that should remain as long as all voices are heard, and none are intentionally silenced. Humanity benefits when humanistic/secular interests, theological concerns, and scientific observations come together in order to paint a larger picture. Later, while Charlie and Janice are in each other's arms, the narrator says, "How sad it was with Harry now, they [Janice and Harry] had become locked rooms to each other, they could hear each other cry but couldn't get in …" (*Rabbit Redux*, 55). This passage is just one more example of Rabbit's separation from humanity as well as our separation from one another.

The day after the restaurant and movie, Rabbit learns of Janice's affair with Charlie. Rabbit reacts by encouraging the affair. He tells Janice, "'Keep him, if he makes you happy. I don't seem to, so go ahead, until you've had your fill at least'" (*Rabbit Redux*, 70). Harry's response is crucial in two ways. First, it supports Arendt's belief that the scientist is constantly finding new Archimedean points to change his world. By encouraging the affair, he induces Janice into taking some action which ultimately forces her out of the house and creates a new point from which Rabbit can change his world. Second, he wants Janice to have the affair so that he can further study Janice's heart. He wants to observe her. What will she do? "Wouldn't you like to keep him?" (*Rabbit Redux*, 70). His encouragement seems cold and indifferent. In the midst of all this conflict between the indifferent Rabbit and his emotional wife, Harry tries to explain to Nelson why his mother cries all the time, "Still? I don't know, kid; she's upset. One thing you must learn about women, their chemistries are different from ours, they cry easier" (*Rabbit Redux,* 73). Here, Harry tries to give a scientific response to explain Janice's emotions. Emotions are strictly chemical. There is no agony of the soul or struggle of the heart. Janice does move out of the house on the same day Apollo 11 touches down, "Apollo Eleven is in lunar orbit and the Eagle is being readied for its historic descent" (*Rabbit Redux,* 81).

The first chapter of *Rabbit, Redux* called, "Pop/Mom/Moon," ends with a long description of the historic conversation between NASA headquarters in Houston and the Apollo 11 crew on the moon. After the long description of the moon landing alternating with details of Harry's family, insight into the Angstrom family is given, and this insight is presented in space terms. The narrator says, " ...the Angstroms still live in the dark half. They prefer it. Sunlight fades. Space kills" (*Rabbit Redux,* 86). This passage presents the belief, similar to that of Arendt, that the end result of space exploration is the death of humankind. Space is inhospitable. It indeed kills.

Updike begins each chapter of *Rabbit, Redux* with an actual, quotation taken from an astronaut during the Apollo missions. In the second chapter called "Jill," Rabbit accepts an invitation from a black co-worker to go to "Jimbo's Lounge." At the bar Harry meets Jill, an eighteen-year-old runaway, who has left her parents and taken up the hippy cause and lifestyle. She is living within the black community. Harry takes her as his lover, and she moves into his home, where she becomes a surrogate sister to Nelson and yet another object for Rabbit to study.

When Harry enters a predominantly black bar, he is consumed with fear but not because he is the only white in the bar. Instead, the fear is the same fear the astronauts probably felt when they stood on the surface of the moon and looked out into the vastness of empty space. Harry is distant from others, and this also reflects how humanity has allowed itself to be distant from one another. Instead of celebrating our differences, we separate ourselves and grow fearful. Updike describes Harry's fear when entering the bar in outer space imagery. This should be all of humanity's fear as well as a fear that needs to be addressed by the church. The fear is not race. The fear is entering the existential expanse of nothingness, "And his inside space expands to include beyond Jimbo's the whole world with its arrowing wars and polychrome races … its strings of gravitational attraction attaching it to every star, its glory in space as of a blue marble swirled with clouds; everything is warm, wet, still coming to birth but himself and his home, which remains a strange dry place, dry and cold and emptily spinning in the void of Penn Villas like a cast-off space capsule" (*Rabbit Redux,* 121). The things that make us human—emotions, spirit, freewill—can easily be cast off into the "dry and cold and emptily spinning" void.

Rabbit leaves the bar with Jill who soon afterwards settles into his home. Here, the group discusses outer space and life on other planets. Jill presents the humanistic argument against space travel, "Without our egos the universe would be absolutely clean, all the animals and rocks and spiders and moon-rocks and stars and grains of sand absolutely doing their thing, unself-consciously" (*Rabbit Redux,* 143). From a humanist perspective, the balance of the universe is in humanity's hands that brings into play an ethical understanding of life. From a Christian perspective, the balance of the universe is in Christ's hands that also bring into play a moral understanding of life and a theological understanding that defines Christ in cosmic terms. Nelson contributes to the discussion by expressing in more simple terms the ultimate demise of humanity in space, "I was thinking, if there was life on other planets, they would have killed our moon men when they stepped out of the space ship. But they didn't so there isn't" (*Rabbit Redux,* 144). Spoken like a lay astrophysicist, Rabbit says to Nelson, "Don't be dumb … The moon is right down our block. We're talking about life in systems billions of light years away" (*Rabbit Redux,* 144). Rabbit finishes the discussion, "Then you better find yourself another universe. The moon is cold, Baby. Cold and ugly. If you [Jill] don't want it, the Commies do. They're   not so fucking proud" (*Rabbit Redux,* 152). The space race between the United States and the Soviet Union was part of the Cold War, a war that nearly destroyed humanity, but also revealed how close technology brought humanity to the brink of destruction through the politics of mutually assured destruction made possible by developing technologies. Religion, even though it has a violent history, cannot destroy the planet. Only science and technology through its ability to split the atom or manipulate and alter viruses can destroy the world several times over.

In the third chapter, Harry returns from work and finds that a black man named Skeeter—who is a militant and a disciple of Malcolm X—has moved into the house because he is running from the police after skipping bail set for a drug-dealing charge. Throughout his stay in Rabbit's home, Skeeter, who calls himself a "Black Jesus," delivers his apocalyptic description of the world. Skeeter tells Rabbit, "We [blacks] are in your dreams. We are *technology's* [emphasis mine] nightmare" (*Rabbit, Redux* 208). Here, Updike may imply that since African-Americans have been oppressed by whites who dominate the scientific community. Skeeter represents the humanist challenging the technological age. He represents the cries of a lost society.

Shortly after Skeeter's move into the home, the four of them—Harry, his son Nelson, Jill, and Skeeter—become one big family, an attempt at perhaps discovering community which is something science or the space program cannot do. However, the community fails; it is an ill-fated attempt because community must be genuine. Harry is cautious about Skeeter, but Harry does not throw Skeeter out of his house, or call the police because Rabbit's urge to study Skeeter is too obsessive. He is willing to jeopardize the well-being of his son and himself and an eighteen-year-old woman in order to meet his need to know. Also, in this third chapter Updike, through the narrator, shows Rabbit as being more sagacious. Harry now understands mathematics. This would have been a uncharacteristic detail in *Rabbit, Run* when Harry was metaphorically conflicted between the scientific era and humanity, "The kid is into algebra this year but can't quite manage that little flip in his head whereby a polynomial cracks open into two nice equalities of x, one minus and one plus" (*Rabbit Redux,* 211). Harry has now embraced the cold, sterile quality of mathematics. Once again, a scientific (mathematical), neutral, indifferent narrative is associated with Rabbit. This represents humanity's narrative as well. As email and text messaging and online *Facebook* accounts continue, the need for face-to-face community diminishes. Only the Church can restore authentic community because it has existing mechanisms to do so.

The chapter focusing on Skeeter has brought much criticism from literary scholar Edward Jackson in his article "Rabbit is Racist." Jackson suggests some form of "repressed homosexuality" (Jackson 444) and racism in the following passage from the novel, "Physically, Skeeter fascinates Rabbit. The lustrous pallor of the tongue and palms and the soles of the feet … Skeeter in his house feels like a finely made electric toy; Harry wants to touch him but is afraid he will get a shock" (*Rabbit Redux*, 221). An alternative reading is that Rabbit is acting on his scientific impulse or his need to study and to know another alien living being. Rabbit's need to know is strong. He wants to investigate. He wants to touch and learn. These are what push science into new frontiers. The question of whether Rabbit is a racist does leave much for debate; however, one thing is sure; Rabbit in fact dehumanizes the people around him by his observations and not by any ill-will. Rabbit represents the mission of the Church, and that is to provide hope, help, and meaning.

At the end of the chapter, Harry's house is burned down, and the police are looking for Skeeter in connection with the fire. Harry finds Skeeter in the back seat of a car and drives the militant to the edge of the county and lets him go. His observations are complete.

In the last chapter of *Rabbit, Redux* called, "Mim," Harry loses his linotype job, forcing his son Nelson and him to move in with his parents in Mount Judge. Midway into the chapter, Rabbit's sister Mim visits their dying mother. During her visit, she sleeps with Charlie Stavros and helps bring Rabbit and Janice back together, a new Archimedean Point.

A crucial scene in the final chapter occurs when Rabbit is laid off from his job and is replaced by a computer. The concern of the Church as well as the humanist hinges on this point. Where will human beings find meaning for their lives when computers and robotics usher in a new, technological era that some how is better because people will no longer have to work. Rabbit's supervisor tells him, "Nothing stands still … We can keep a few men on, retrain them to the computer tape, we've worked the deal out with the union, but this is a sacrifice" (*Rabbit Redux*, 296-97). Ironically, Rabbit is snared by the impulse he chose to follow. He has bought into the belief that technology and science solves all problems, so he accepts the decision to embrace technology, "Rabbit tries to help him. "So no linotypers, huh?" (*Rabbit Redux*, 297). Harry understands the importance of scientific progress, and he willingly sacrifices himself in the name of that progress. Arendt believes the postmodern, technological society destroys the individual because he is no longer needed. Arendt adds that scientists believe computers can do man's work better and more efficiently. She writes, "There are, however, scientists who state that computers can do 'what a human brain cannot comprehend,' and this is an ... alarming proposition" (Arendt, 269). Here, Arendt expresses her concern over the scientists' idea for using the computers. She believes computers are merely tools to be used by people not a device to replace them.

During Mim's visit, Rabbit and his sister discuss his marriage problems and what Mim has learned of Janice's feelings toward Rabbit, after she slept with Stavros. Mim tells Rabbit that Stavros is probably the first person to give Janice attention in thirty years. Harry responds to Mim by saying, "[Charlie] 'must use a microscope'" (*Rabbit Redux*, 318). "Microscope" is an important choice of words, describing one possibility of how humanity may be understood or observed—by studying fluid on a side. Rabbit is using a metaphorical microscope to study those around him. He continues to separate himself from people as if he is gazing through the lens of a microscope at some single-cell creature which creates a real disconnect between Rabbit and the rest of humanity. One of the roles the Church must fulfill is to connect people in a meaningful way by creating community to bring people together not socially isolating them, and here is where science fails.

Before *Rabbit, Redux* comes to an end, Updike uses one last scientific narration to be associated with Rabbit. Updike writes, "Harry was always worrying about how wide the world was, caring about things like how far stars are and the moon shot ..." (*Rabbit Redux*, 332). Notice, he does not care about people only the vast emptiness of space now holds his attention. Once again a Rabbit novel ends with Harry and Janice getting back together; in *Rabbit Redux*, similar to *Rabbit, Run*, he returns to a new wife, "She [Janice] is harder to bully now" (*Rabbit Redux*, 338). Rabbit is returning to a new and different world, i.e. a new fulcrum or Archimedean Point. Janice has had an affair and is more independent. She in fact has more control over her life than Rabbit because she knows what she wants; whereas, Harry only wants to observe and study.

Rabbit Redux, as in *Rabbit, Run*, has several references to celestial bodies that bridge the beginning and end of the books. But in *Rabbit Redux* Updike frequently inserts references to an artificial world of plastic and chemicals. This is the world humanity has inherited, a world devoid of flesh and blood.

Robert Detweiler, in his book *John Updike*, addresses the space imagery as being a dominant component of the Rabbit novels. The space images, such as the fragments of recorded American and Russian astronaut dialogue scattered throughout *Rabbit Redux*, are presented historically and accurately, and additional images of outer space are found throughout the book by means of televised news coverage of the moon landing in order to drive home the dominant role of science in American society. Science is in the forefront as well as the background of society; it is every where. (Detweiler, 155). Detweiler writes, "The spectral figures of the astronauts on the moon set the tone for the strong ghost imagery, which stands for the insubstantial quality of American life and the haunting memory of better times" (Detweiler, 155). Detweiler points out the great disconnect between the U.S. space program and the average citizen. "The strong ghost imagery" that Detweiler poignantly describes the ultimate death of humanity somewhere in the universe's vastness. The Church's role is to adopt a "cosmic Christ" belief system in order to counter-balance a strict scientific approach to the universe. By doing so, people can find meaning and purpose, while science can only add to the vault of knowledge without inadvertently destroying what it means to be human. The Church must move away from the notion of personal salvation toward an understanding of cosmic renewal and rebirth. This connects humanity to all Creation thus giving people meaning within the vastness of the universe in which humanity is beginning to explore. Also, by taking Detweiler's quotation one step further in reading the imagery in Arendt's terms, one may argue that the "better times" Detweiler discusses is the time period before space exploration and the atomic bomb [a time before the possibility of mutual, world-wide destruction]. For Rabbit, this "better time" occurred during his high school basketball days. Today, computers, email, the world-wide web, smart phones have become essentials to every day life. Is this the better life?

In addition to the constant statements about Harry being surrounded by space, other passages directly associated with Rabbit connect him to space travel and celestial bodies. At the beginning of the novel when Rabbit is about to leave the bar, the narrator says, "Put the metal on the moon" (*Rabbit Redux,* 19). In most of *Rabbit Redux,* through the voices of Rabbit's son Nelson and the narrator, updates on the lunar mission's status show or demonstrate how it has become a part of Rabbit's life. Nelson tells his father that "They've left earth's orbit! They're forty-three thousand miles away," (*Rabbit Redux,* 23) and later, "The astronauts are nearing the moon's gravitational influence" (*Rabbit Redux,* 58). In other words, through science and technology, a great divide or gulf has emerged—43,000 miles now separate people.

Amidst all this description of travel to the moon, Skeeter presence to Rabbit the biblical notion of creation and mixes it with the Big Bang Theory. This combination best describes where Americans are in their understanding of how the world came into being. Harry thinks in terms of space metaphors when he is around Skeeter and when his house is on fire. Outer space gets associated with destruction. Humanity's demise is somewhere in the universe: Skeeter is an unpredictable, destructive force, and the house fire consumes all. In regards to the house fire and when Rabbit first learns of some emergency underway at his home, Updike writes, "The universe is unsleeping, neither ants nor stars sleep, to die will be forever wide awake" (*Rabbit Redux,* 276), and " …the house fire pulls on Rabbit like 'Jupiter's gravitational pull'" (*Rabbit Redux,* 281). Skeeter and the house fire force Rabbit off his Archimedean point to another fulcrum. Once again, Rabbit is constantly moving from point to point. He is searching. He is investigating his world for the best options, but the more he searches or investigates, the more his humanity is diminished or lost.

In keeping with Updike's concern with the role of science/technological in society and with its potential for harm, he makes several references to an artificial world which only adds to the reality of a dying humanity. The narrator and the characters describe an unnatural world full of chemicals. Janice tells her husband, "'They [women] all go to bed now without even being asked, everybody's on the Pill, they just assume it'" (*Rabbit Redux,* 62), and later, " …nothing [made] straight from a human hand, furniture Rabbit has lived among but never known, made of substances he cannot name …" (*Rabbit Redux,* 69-70). This artificial world presents itself when Rabbit is shopping for a gift for his mother, "What can a dying person desire?

Grotesque prosthetic devices—arms, legs, battery-operated hearts—run through Rabbit's head as he and Nelson as he and Nelson walk the dazzling, Sunday-stilled downtown of Brewer" (*Rabbit Redux,* 84). This synthetic world is also present in the pub while Rabbit is drinking an alcoholic beverage, "He [Rabbit] sips the Stinger but now it tastes chemical like the bottom of that milkshake" (*Rabbit Redux,* 111). These passages describe a world created by the scientist. This world is devoid of human touch, and there is a separation of humanity from creation. There is a gulf between people as well as the natural world. Granted, Updike sets out to record the history of the last three decades, but he, like Arendt, sees the Apollo 11 mission as the one scientific discovery that threatens human stature because the farther we go into space the less the significance of humanity and definitely the Church, for it will directly challenge everything people believe about God. Rabbit's desire to metaphorically conquer space is the reason his character in *Rabbit Redux* has been called a racist, a womanizer, and a stoic. Rabbit is not those labels; he is an indifferent observer, like a scientist, and Rabbit represents the uncaring, "scientific" community. The Church is about flesh and blood community, and how race, gender, sexual orientation, ethnicity, and nationality strengthens community and should be celebrated as a gift and not a phenomenon to be studied. Community is at the heart of the Church. Science has improved the quality of life of people through such things as medical advancements; likewise, the Church improves the quality of life by bringing diverse people together in support of one another. This distinction is essential for the betterment of humanity. The formation of community is a crucial role of the Church in the 21st Century if it is to remain relevant. There must be both positive scientific improvements directly pertaining to people's lives, and community must be in place to assure personal fulfillment.

If one assumes that Rabbit is following his scientific impulse in the second novel, several questions about Harry's character and behaviors are answered: Harry encourages his wife to have an affair because he has separated himself from humanity, and he wants to observe or study what happens. He invites Jill and Skeeter into his home in order to study them. Updike uses images of the Apollo 11 mission throughout the book because Rabbit sympathizes with the astronauts because of their distance from humanity. Rabbit is exploring—from the scientific point of view—the void, the *Event Horizon*.

In *Rabbit Is Rich*, John Updike continues documenting post-World War II United States and its scientific advancement. The first two novels, *Rabbit, Run* and *Rabbit Redux*, placed Harry Angstrom in the context of the 1950s and 1960s, times when he was struggling with his humanistic urges and the "pseudo-scientific" aspect of his nature as fueled by a science-dominated culture. By the third novel, *Rabbit Is Rich,* the year is 1979, and Rabbit, as in *Rabbit Redux*, is still acting as the metaphorical "scientist." Now he is clearly observing and separating himself from humanity, but toward the end of this third novel Harry Angstrom goes to the "void" described by Hannah Arendt and returns a different, more humanistic man. His near *Event Horizon* almost destroys him, but he manages to come back from the void a changed man. In *Rabbit Is Rich*, the reader sees Harry Angstrom subtly making a 360-degree change in his life. In *Rabbit, Run*, Harry displayed traces of humanism. His humanistic side was aborted by the failure of both his marriage and career. However, the accidental death of his daughter provided the impetus to leave humanity behind and go with the "scientific" urges that were prevalent throughout *Rabbit Redux*. He can disappear into the vastness of space like an astronaut.

Rabbit is now forty-six years old, and he lives during a time when the United States is "Running out of gas," and people know the "great American ride is ending" (*Rabbit Is Rich*, 3), or the very essence of humanity disappearing. He is riding on the financial coat tails of his wife Janice, who has also changed, and his mother in law, who has accumulated considerable wealth by owning and managing Springer Motors, a car sales lot. Janice has changed by gaining the respect of her own husband and is in control of her life. As indicated by his interest in economics and investments, Harry has, likewise, changed. On the first page of the novel, Updike introduces a new characteristic of Rabbit. Harry now reads *Consumer Reports*, and "For the first time since childhood Rabbit is happy, simply, to be alive" (*Rabbit Is Rich*, 10), but " …he avoids mirrors, when he used to love them" (*Rabbit Is Rich*, 6). Humanity fails to take a long, hard look at itself.

Is Rabbit really happy? Rabbit's avoidance of mirrors indicates he does not like what he sees. He, like the state of humanity, thinks he is satisfied because he equates happiness and power with money and economics, but throughout *Rabbit Is Rich*, many allusions and direct references to death make Harry struggle with his own mortality. Science can explain death, but explanation is no comfort to a dying person or a grieving family. One facing one's mortality must feel connected to humanity in order not to die alone. This is the place of the Church. Added to his fear of death, Janice and Ma Springer have "castrated" Rabbit by taking away his decision making ability, i.e. power, at Springer Motors. This castration humbles him. Harry's first step toward happiness begins shortly after his epiphany near the end of this third novel, when he realizes there is more to life than money, but it takes entering the void of human existence, which Arendt prophesied about the finality of science, to discover his happiness. In other words, for Harry\Rabbit to regain his humanity, he must hit rock bottom and discover that he actually needs humanity to survive. Science cannot solve all his problems. He needs the human touch.

As in *Rabbit Redux*, Updike begins with a long, gloom and doom narration about the state of affairs in the United States, "People are going wild, their dollars are going rotten, they shell out like there's no tomorrow" (*Rabbit Is Rich*, 3). While working on the lot, Harry turns to his best friend Charlie Stavros and says, "Did you see in the paper the other day where some station owner and his wife ... were pumping gas for a line and one of the cars slips its clutch and crushes the wife against the car next in line, broke her hip ... and while the husband was holding her and begging for help the people in the cars instead of giving him any help took over the pumps and gave themselves free gas?" (*Rabbit Is Rich*, 7).

The above disturbing and graphic information describes a direct critique by Updike on science and technology. People have been enslaved by the financial costs of keeping up with technological development, and they have been dehumanized by machines, in this case cars, and have lost all compassion or that which makes them human by failing to help the woman with the broken hip. People have become uncaring; it is here where the Church is best suited to re-instruct people on the need for kindness and compassion in community. The Church is not perfect and has demonstrated its imperfection throughout the ages; however, the basic tools for change remain in place. This graphic image at the gas station only exemplifies the dehumanizing effect of science on humanity and is further illustrated a few pages later when a young man, accompanied by a woman who could be Harry's daughter as a result of his affair with Ruth in *Rabbit, Run*, comes into the car showroom, "The pair comes in shyly, like elongated animals, sniffing the air-conditioned air" (*Rabbit Is Rich,* 13). Rabbit, after showing the couple several Toyotas, wants to ask the girl, "And is your mother's name Ruth? Harry wants to ask, but doesn't, lest he frighten her, and destroy for himself the vibration of excitement, of possibility untested" (*Rabbit Is Rich,* 22). This look into Harry's "scientific" psyche is a throw-back to his scientific treatment of Skeeter, Jill, and Nelson in the second novel. He saw them as animals to be studied, creatures separate from himself that are subjects to be tested. Technology is only increasing that insensitivity in this postmodern age.

Rabbit's insensitivity toward humanity is prevalent throughout most of the novel. After he leaves the lot for home, cars pass him at high rates of speed. Harry thinks to himself, "Maybe they'll kill themselves on a telephone pole in the next mile. He hopes so" (*Rabbit Is Rich,* 34). When Harry gets home, "…he goes down the brick back steps into the grateful space" (*Rabbit Is Rich,* 46). The words "grateful space" indicates that Harry thinks he belongs in space, and according to Arendt, space is the ultimate destiny for the scientist which becomes humanity's final demise, but not in the sense of annihilation but rather isolation from the universe, creation/world, and one another.

During this brief scene in Harry's home, the reader learns that Harry and Janice live with Ma Springer, and they are members of a country club, where Janice manages to keep her "young" figure by playing tennis, and Rabbit continues his golf game there on a regular basis. His golf game has changed considerably since he started playing with Rev. Eccles in *Rabbit, Run*. He now looks at the scientific side of the game; whereas, in *Rabbit, Run* he simply hit the ball. While in bed that night, Rabbit thinks about hitting the golf ball at the club, "Arms like ropes, he tells himself sometimes, with considerable success, and then, when that goes bad, Shift the weight. Or, Don't chicken wing it, or, keep the angle, meaning the angle between club and arms when wrists are cocked (*Rabbit Is Rich,* 50). Rabbit is applying science to improve his golf game which represents his life, but he still is slicing the ball—science has failed him. He does not care. His postmodern faith in science cannot be broken.

At the Flying Eagle Club, Updike introduces important characters who will lead Rabbit to his humanistic epiphany: Webb and Cindy Murkett and Ronnie and Thelma Harrison are sitting around a table drinking, and the group starts swapping stories. Cindy is discussing astrology, "It's no trick, it's ancient science. It's the most ancient science there is" (*Rabbit Is Rich,* 62). Amidst this conversation, Rabbit thinks about his ex-lover Ruth and wondering whether that girl who came to the car lot was his daughter or not. Harry continues to have biological interests in his offspring.

Janice and Harry, while at the club, get a telephone call from Ma Springer who informs them that Nelson, now a student at Kent State University, is coming home from a trip to Colorado, and he is bringing his friend, Melanie. Shortly after Nelson's arrival, Nelson tells his father all the places he has been; Rabbit is proud of Nelson's ability and desire to travel, and the narrator metaphorically says, "Places where Rabbit has never been--his blood has traveled for him, along the tracks of his dreams" (*Rabbit Is Rich,* 75). Rabbit approves of Nelson's constant movement; also, this symbolizes Rabbit's need to carry his genes into the future, and once again it shows how the scientists' need, according to Arendt, to travel out into space and find new Archimedean points has pierced Rabbit to his marrow. It is a part of his existence that was passed on to Nelson. A few pages later additional insight into Harry's "scientific" psyche is revealed by narration, "He sees nothing of himself there [in Nelson's face] except the small straight nose and a cowlick in one eyebrow that sends a little fan of hairs the wrong way and seems to express a doubt. Amazing, genes. So precise in all that coiled coding they can pick up a tiny cowlick like that" (*Rabbit Is Rich,* 79). Humanity gets reduced to "genes' and "coiled coding," which is the role of science. This role is dangerous if it is not tempered by the belief that there is something immeasurable and unobservable about the human spirit. People are more than genetic sequencing and chemicals interacting in such a way that evoke certain behaviors. The place and role of humanity are important to one's existence. Studies have been conducted examining the chemical reactions in the brain to religious experience. What will be the point of human existence if everything can be reduced to chemistry? Notice, Harry does not see Nelson with the fondness of a parent because it is all about genes. Obviously, the "coiled coding" is a description of DNA, the substance that stores genetic information. This type of narration or description would not have been associated with Rabbit in *Rabbit, Run* because, as mentioned previously, Rabbit was still struggling with himself in the first novel. Along with the scientific description, such as the DNA, Updike continues with the concept of Rabbit finding Arendt's Archimedean point, to try and improve his world. Harry says, "I've always been curious about the South: love hot weather'" (*Rabbit Is Rich,* 82). In the first three Rabbit novels, the South represents an oasis, a place where Harry can be at peace [This idea of movement or going to the South becomes significant in the final Rabbit novel, *Rabbit At Rest,* in which Harry finds his resting place]. It is seen as the final Archimedean Point.

Updike continues to develop in this third novel Rabbit's "scientific" psyche. For example, Harry's anxiety over getting maple sap on his car illustrates a common notion held by many post-Industrial Revolution philosophers that humanity will become enslaved by technology. Arendt goes so far as to say humanity could die. Maple sap is the life force of trees, so without it, trees would die; thus, he is rejecting life. Harry obsesses over the upkeep of his automobiles. His fondness for his cars exceeds his feelings for Nelson, his own son. He loves material things more than his flesh and blood. Technology creates a material environment. One must accumulate more and more technology in order to remain relevant. The material exceeds the spiritual. From a Christian perspective, then, how can we appreciate the flesh and blood of Christ in a synthetic, technological-lifestyle world? Many churches are split over "alternative lifestyles," such as homosexual and trans-gendered. Those are not the problem. The real problems churches are facing come from the technological lifestyle. Technological devices become an extension of the individual. This forces him or her to become a slave to material gain.

Furthermore, Updike can be direct in using narration of a scientific nature to further describe Harry's psyche. During a dinner party to which Stavros, Janice's former lover, is invited, Updike writes, "Rabbit sees the phenomenon as he would something else in Nature—a Japanese beetle on a leaf, or two limbs of a tree rubbing together in the wind. Then he remembers, descending into the molecules, what love feels like, huge, skin on skin, planets impinging" (*Rabbit Is Rich*, 94). This is a direct connection to how Rabbit observes the world. As the Rabbit novels progress through history, one sees Rabbit becoming more and more seduced by scientific discovery. This passage is a throwback to *Rabbit Redux*, when Rabbit was busy observing Skeeter and Jill. When Stavros enters the Springer-Angstrom home, he becomes the "phenomenon" mentioned in the passage, and Rabbit, being the "scientist," observes this phenomenon as a scientist who studies the macro-world around him. He also observes the situation on the microcosm level by "descending into the molecules." While Harry—*Everyman* of the postmodern world who is rooted in science—is making his unconscious, scientific observation, he is thinking of love, indicating that love is not felt or experienced but is to be observed like any other phenomenon. Love is like two "planets impinging" on one another. Updike's use of "impinging" suggests some type of burden love places on people, and his use of "planets" is similar to the importance scientists place on conquering space, according to Arendt. Updike further reinforces this notion that space exploration is the way to go for saving humankind, "He [Rabbit] prefers them [cashews] salted, soaked in sodium, but got this kind in deference to Melanie, he's being brainwashed about chemicals. Still, some chemicals must have entered into this freeze-drying too, there's nothing you can eat won't hurt you down here on Earth" (*Rabbit Is Rich*, 96). The fragment, "nothing you can eat won't hurt you down here on Earth," suggests the Earth is becoming a dangerous place to live. The constant pursuit of technology to be used in every day life leads people to want more and more of it. Once one jumps into the technological river, he or she is pushed farther down the river. For example, BETA and VCRs were no longer sufficient, so they were replaced by DVD players. Now, blue ray is replacing the DVD. With each advancement, there comes additional financial burdens—software must be purchased regularly to keep one's personal computer up to date.

After Updike presents these scientific descriptions and references to space, he writes these words, " …the darkening space of the porch. Alien. Moonracker" (*Rabbit Is Rich*, 98), Updike reveals a humanistic and tender side to Harry. He is about to eat at the party: "Harry doesn't like to be reminded that these are living things, with eyes and hearts, that we eat ..." (*Rabbit Is Rich*, 104). Here, it is clear to resist any attempt to fully demonize science because it plays an important role raising the quality of life. Religion must understand and accept that; however, science must understand that religion and humanism, too, can play an important role in raising the quality of life. This brief but different look into Rabbit's psyche quickly changes when he finds out Nelson has scrapped his Toyota (*Rabbit Is Rich*, 105). Harry is furious with Nelson for damaging his property; Rabbit expresses real anger, "He wants to put his hands on the boy, whether to give him a push or comfort his instinct is obscure; the actual touch might prove which, but Nelson stays just ahead of his father's fingertips, dodging into the summer night (*Rabbit Is Rich*, 106). He wants to comfort his son or kill him, but he can no longer rely on his instincts because his scientific impulse has suppressed what it means to be truly human , truly a father. Nelson responds to his father by saying, "Dad, it's just a thing; you're looking like you lost your best friend" (*Rabbit Is Rich*, 107). Nelson's response accentuates Harry's enslavement to technology.

Furthermore, enslavement to technology creates distance between people, like isolated planets spinning alone in the darkness. Nelson describes his father's lack of care for the people around him as distant as space. Nelson tells Melanie, "He is bad, really bad. He doesn't know what's up, and he doesn't care, and he thinks he's so great" (*Rabbit Is Rich*, 134). Nelson is right in telling his friend that his father does not care because at this point in his life Rabbit—driven by his "scientific" impulse—cannot lose his objectivity. Nelson thinks his father is happy, but he is not. Now, more than ever, Rabbit is concerned with death and his own existence. Issues of death and dying fall into the realm of the spiritual. Science can offer only a limited understanding by simply describing the physiological dimensions of death.

After Nelson's "uncaring" description of his father, Harry, Janice, and Ma Springer go to the Poconos—where Harry takes up swimming, tennis and running—for a vacation. While playing tennis with Janice, Harry begins to show some change in his character: a change eventually putting him back in touch with his humanistic side. Updike writes, "The (tennis) ball arcs back steadily from her (Janice) racket while he hits it too hard or else, trying to `stroke' it like she tells him, pops it weakly into the net. 'Harry, don't try to steer it,' she says. 'Keep your knees bent. Point your hip toward the net.' She has had a lot of lessons. The decade past has taught her more than it has taught him (*Rabbit Is Rich,* 138).

This passage is more than just a description of a tennis match. Janice counsels Harry to live his life and to abandon his old ways. She tells her husband "don't try to steer it;" in other words, Harry should not try to control his surroundings or world. She also advises him to keep his knees bent, and by bending his knees that puts Harry closer to the Earth and out of space. Through tennis Janice forces Rabbit to examine himself, "What has he done, he wonders as he waits to receive the serve, with this life of his more than half over?" The narrator continues, " … Harry had kicked against death, then he gave in and went to work." Here, Rabbit begins to realize his own mortality, a realization putting him in touch with the world and not outer space, "He loves the treetops about their heads, and the August blue above these." These issues of life are life only addressed by religion. Furthermore, Harry admits to his own ignorance; whereas before he noticed nature's phenomenon, "He loves nature, though he can name almost nothing in it" (*Rabbit Is Rich,* 139). The narrator shows how Rabbit begins to appreciate humankind, "What a threadbare thing we make of life! Yet what a marvelous thing the mind is, they [scientists] can't make a machine like it, though some of these computers Ed was telling about fill rooms; and the body can do a thousand things there isn't a factory in the world can duplicate the motion (*Rabbit Is Rich,* 139). Rabbit's praise of the mind and body is a new revelation in his psyche, and while he is out jogging in the Poconos he has a brief vision of Arendt's void. The narrator says "The dead stare upwards," and among the dead he sees Skeeter who "turns his face away." Harry begins to see all the dead people who he once knew, "…he imagines, like stars, and beyond them there are myriads, whole races like the Cambodians, that have drifted into death" (*Rabbit Is Rich,* 141). All indicates there is a place for humanistic and religious pursuits in the world despite increasing presence of science and technology in the lives of individuals.

A similar scene is repeated when the Angstroms and Ma Springer return from their vacation, and Janice and Rabbit go to the country club, except here Updike presents more tenderness in Rabbit. Updike says, "Harry contemplates his empty glass," or this can be read as a questioning of his existence (*Rabbit Is Rich*, 177). Updike continues with Rabbit's pensive behavior by noting, "When he contemplates it [his empty glass or life] by himself, bringing a person into the world seems as terrible as pushing somebody into a furnace. By the time they finally get out onto the golf course, green seems a shade of black [void]. Every blade of grass at his feet is an individual life that will die [because of the scientific impulse of man], that has flourished to no purpose ... his feet blankets the dead (*Rabbit Is Rich*, 177). Humans may go out into the universe, but there they will always die. Death is a part of life. Science tries to disrupt the natural cycle of life and death by seeking a genetic fountain of youth. The pronoun "it" can be read as a replacement for Rabbit's empty glass, or Harry is actually contemplating his own existence. The words "a shade of black" suggest the blackness or utter darkness of outer space, and the reference to "die" suggests that once man has entered that darkness in the universe he will die. This second death section also reveals an unprecedented caring side to Harry, "One of the weaknesses of Harry's [golf] game [life] is he cannot make himself take a divot, he tries with misapplied tenderness ..." (*Rabbit Is Rich*, 178). Rabbit is trying to reclaim his humanity as are all people whether they are aware of it or not. The Church can help in this re-connection process.

The references to death are not only found in the two sections previously discussed, but death is scattered throughout much of the first half of the novel, "When you think of the dead, you got to be grateful" (*Rabbit Is Rich*, 4); "It gives him (Rabbit) pleasure ... to contemplate the world's wasting, to know that the earth is mortal too" (*Rabbit Is Rich*, 12); " ...the hospitals keeping people alive that are really dead like some game they're playing at Medicaid's expense ... " (*Rabbit Is Rich*, 29). Midway through *Rabbit Is Rich* the allusions to death are different, "Fred Springer made that long climb into the tree of the stars. Lost in space" (*Rabbit Is Rich*, 188), and "He (Rabbit) feels the house swell beneath him ... the dead awakened, Skeeter, Pop, Mom Mr. Abendroth" (*Rabbit Is Rich*, 189). Now for Rabbit, death becomes personal, and he continues to realize his own mortality, which sets him up for his encounter with the void, or his own *Event Horizon* in which he may or may not escape.

Why are all these references to death important? The descriptions get to the heart of the matter. What is technology's effect on humanity? First, they show that Harry has not completely abandoned his humanistic character revealed in *Rabbit, Run*, when he played basketball, and the death imagery further illustrates the debate/dichotomy in Rabbit's heart which is also present in the first novel. Second, they reveal a tender side to Rabbit that had not been explored in the previous two novels; Harry's constant contemplation of death shows his new maturity because he now thinks only of his family and his own existence. The final reason is the most important. The references to death similar to those of space and space travel in *Rabbit, Run* and *Rabbit Redux* serve to link Harry's "scientific" urges to the fundamental struggle of humanity in a technological age. Humans are faces with difficult choices: everyone benefits by the majority of scientific advancement and technological improvements of daily life. However, the reality of nuclear, biological, and chemical destruction looms in our collective psyche. That is the struggle of the heart that William Faulkner describes in his Nobel Peace Prize for literature. Faulkner believes that even in an age when planetary annihilation is possible as a result of nuclear war, the only true battle is waged within the heart. Updike further traces this theme connecting science to growing isolation.

Rabbit, Run alludes to humanity gazing into the universe searching for a new Archimedean point with constant descriptions of celestial bodies. *Rabbit Redux* refers to the Apollo 11 mission and space flight, which illustrate humanity's actual movement into space, and the diminishing of humanity's stature in the universe. When humanity is considered an important component of the universe, then, governments are less likely to bring about humanity's destruction. *Rabbit Is Rich* alludes to death, which is similar to Arendt's point that the ultimate ends to space travel is the void in the universe, and for Updike this equates with death. These three novels demonstrate Arendt's concept of humanity's metaphorical shifting Archimedean point to constantly advance itself; however, Heisenberg's Uncertainty Principal, as well as concepts like chaos theory, loom in the future. The plight of humanity is best exemplified by Rabbit as *Everyman*. The first fulcrum or point that science lays its fulcrum is the study of Earth itself as shown in *Rabbit, Run*; then, humanity moves into space, as illustrated by Apollo 11 in

Rabbit Redux, to find a new point, fulcrum of change, but humanity cannot stop at the moon, or in another words, knowledge will not end there. In an infinite universe, inevitably science will perceive there is not enough room on the moon, and so, it must move out into space only to find Arendt's void, the end of humanity. This is described in *Rabbit Is Rich* as death.

Harry's pensiveness over death gives the reader a look into the humanistic side of Rabbit's psyche, but the look is brief. When Harry returns from his vacation to the Poconos, he reverts to his metaphorical, "scientific" impulse as evident in the narration. While Rabbit is driving [moving] in his car and listening to the radio he thinks, " ...life may exist, some scientists are coming to believe, on Titan, Saturn's largest moon (*Rabbit Is Rich,* 181)." Rabbit's oscillation between science and humanism reflects all our movements back and forth between what is of flesh and blood and what is of microchip and plastic. We are at the crossroads where science, humanism, and religion converge, making for confusing times. Furthermore, "Harry is fascinated by fags, what makes them tick, why they have done this to themselves" (*Rabbit Is Rich,* 191). This sentence makes the reader aware that Harry likes to study the world around him; much like a scientist, he wants to know what makes things "tick." Science's constant pursuit of what makes us "tick," i.e. finding genetic causes for the things we do, is slowly pushing religion to the side.

Above we see how Rabbit reverts to his "scientific" nature, but he is not left untouched by the humanistic visions he had while jogging in the Poconos. Those same visions return while he is running on Brewer's city streets, "He is running along Porter Avenue now, still uphill, saving the downhill for the homeward leg, along the gutter where the water from the ice plant used to run, an edge of green slime, life tries to get a grip anywhere, on earth that is not on the moon, that's another thing he doesn't like about the thought of climbing through the stars" (*Rabbit Is Rich,* 226). The discovery of life outside of earth will diminish humanity's stature in the universe, challenging many religious/theological beliefs. Of course, the other thing he clearly does not like about "climbing through the stars" is death. This is the first critical passage in the novel directly attacking space travel, but within the paragraph a dichotomy, i.e. conflicted humanity, exists. The narrator is obviously criticizing voyaging out into space, but on the other hand Rabbit is running "uphill" toward the sky. In *Rabbit, Run*, when Harry was running from his daughter's funeral, he was running uphill, and at that point in the novel he abandoned his humanistic side and acted as the metaphorical "scientist," but in the passage now under consideration Harry is "saving the downhill for the homeward leg," which indicates a return to earth or to humanity. He is coming home. Updike further describes this scene by writing, "Then second wind comes and you break free into a state where your body does it by itself, a machine being ridden, your brain like the astronaut in the tip of the rocket … "(*Rabbit Is Rich*, 229). This passage would seem to contradict the previous one criticizing space travel, but in fact the two are complementary. Updike is praising the human body and its ability to "break free." The body is sleek like the design of a rocket, and it is directed/ guided by a remarkable brain or control center.

Basically, what Updike has described up to this point is the conflicted nature of the postmodern man and woman. All of humanity, including the Church, is in a transitional period. They are running up hill to run from itself. Part of humanity still embraces the Earth—nature, religion, art, music, philosophy, and so forth, but Humanity is on a slippery slope headed toward oblivion. The reader again is shown a tender side to Harry, such as the description while he is running, but that image is destroyed when Nelson wrecks a second car on the eve of his and Pru's wedding, and Harry says "'Oh no. That son of a bitch. That little son of a bitch'" (*Rabbit Is Rich*, 232). Harry's lack of understanding and compassion on one hand and his sincere concern for humanity and his own mortality on the other hand leave him in a state of fear and confusion. During the wedding reception, a conversation between his wife Janice's former lover, Stravos, forces Rabbit to look inside himself for meaning, "A rock in space, is the image these words bring to Rabbit's mind. He is interested in space, and scans the paper every day for more word on these titanic quasars on the edge of everything, and in the Sunday section studies the new up-close photos of Jupiter, expecting to spot a clue that all those scientists have missed; God might have a few words to say yet. In the vacuum of the heart love falls forever" (*Rabbit Is Rich*, 271).

It is difficult for Rabbit to abandon his humanity; moreover, he thinks that if one behaves like "a rock in space"—cold, hard, dark—he is isolated from the world and cannot be hurt, this makes Rabbit "interested in space." As Rabbit reads the newspaper to find more information on the "titanic quasars on the edge of everything," recalling Arendt's point about humanity's desire to go to the edge of the universe only to lose its humanity—the end game is humanity's destruction. This is where the Church gives meaning.

Harry makes one last unconscious effort to maintain his "scientific" character, to be the postmodern *Everyman.*. The Angstroms and the Harrisons are at the Murkett's home for food, alcohol and conversation. Harry, acting like the archaeologist, goes through the Murkett's bathroom medicine closet searching for "Certain mysterious artifacts ..." that will help Rabbit understand Cindy Murkett because he wants to have sex with her. Eventually, he goes to their other bathroom, located off the bedroom, and searches for more items in "a cavernous space, forbidden" (*Rabbit Is Rich,* 305). He finds in the drawer of their night stand photographs of the nude Murketts making love; this is followed by a long description of the photographs. The scene ends with all three couples discussing taking a trip to the Caribbean in January.

This final encounter with Harry's "scientific" nature has significance for understanding modernity's confrontation with a scientific age. During the Murkett's party, the party where Harry looked through the Murkett's personal belongings, the Angstroms, Harrisons and Murketts agree to vacation together in the Bahamas. The section begins with the couples entering the airplane. Upon arrival, the couples do the typical tourist activities of dancing, drinking and swimming. There is a brief narration about space when Webb Murkett, "who knows stars from his years in the Navy," points out galaxies and constellations, such as the Big Dipper and Southern Cross, to the group (*Rabbit Is Rich,* 395). The couples continue swimming, sailing, and playing golf, but the vacation changes when the women begin tossing around the idea of swapping marital partners for one evening. The first night the women pick their male partners and the men have their choice the second night. Harry wants Cindy Murkett, but Thelma Harrison chooses him instead.

All the space imagery—void/emptiness, death, darkness, and outer space—and the movement/running imagery found in *Rabbit, Run, Rabbit Redux,* and *Rabbit Is Rich* lead up to this one sexually graphic scene when Rabbit and Thelma are in bed, and where they have anal intercourse. It is described as a disappearance into a void—"there is no sensation in the void, pure black box of nothingness. He is in that void ..." (*Rabbit Is Rich,* 417). The graphic description is essential in order to make the point that when humanity loses its emotional and relational connection with one another—as demonstrated by the spouse swapping—humanity disappears into the void. Humanity, depreciates marginalizes, and isolates itself. The Church can re-establish those connections if it carries out what it was called to do in the gospels, the formation of a caring community.

Harry Angstrom has been a perfect example of Arendt's secular criticism of how science affects humanity in general and the individual specifically. Arendt uses space exploration as a way to demonstrate how science destroys humanity. She believes the scientist constantly moves forward without regard for consequences to try and change the world. It is not the movement forward that is the problematic because one cannot go backwards. It is the lack of responsibility or checks and balances that raises concerns. The final point humanity will encounter is the nothingness of outer space, which will be the demise of humanity because the true insignificance of humanity will be suddenly realized. In the spouse swapping scene, Updike presents an accurate description of a void, "a pure black box, a casket of nothingness". The "black box" and "nothingness" describes outer space; a place where there is "no sensation," or in other words, a place where humanity has no feelings. And the use of the word, "casket," associates this "nothingness" with the death or the end of humanity. Rabbit's constant running in the three novels places him in that metaphorical void of outer space. Harry enters that void and returns a changed man: with every new scientific-advancement, we, too, return changed. While in a department store, people on their cellular phones talk about their private affairs while shopping. In this postmodern era people have cried out for their rights to privacy, but technology is the one taking away those rights. Technology has changed our sense of privacy consciously or unconsciously, and technology forces us to abandon that sense of privacy.

Fortunately for humanity, the results of Rabbit's near encounter with the void are positive. He has returned which means it is not too late for humanity and the Church. Science/technology can and will always play an important role in this return when balanced with humanistic and theological concerns. Rabbit is now in touch with himself and the world around him; he can talk to Ruth without running away. Rabbit no longer runs. In the final Rabbit novel, *Rabbit At Rest*, Harry is truly happy and has found his earthly center in Florida. *Rabbit Is Rich* ends with Harry holding his granddaughter, "Through all this she has pushed to be here, in his lap, his hands, a real presence hardly weighing anything but alive. Fortune's hostage, heart's desire, a granddaughter. His. Another nail in his coffin" (*Rabbit Is Rich,* 467). This is the last sentence of the book. The reader sees a tender side to Rabbit. He finally realizes the importance of human life and the struggle of humanity. He now knows that science cannot control or regulate humanity. Science cannot research the heart, soul, and spirit. It tries to come up with genetic and evolutionary reasons why people do what they do. Furthermore, there is always the Black Swan. The Black Swan theory as proposed by Nassim Nicholas Taleb refers to a rare but major, unpredictable impact event beyond the realm of normal expectations. These are events of such magnitude that they have large historical, consequences. Science cannot predict it. The Church has an answer for this—the mystery of God. As long as there are people, there will be a Black Swan from time to time, and science cannot account for this which means even science is not one hundred percent trustworthy, and humanity must always be skeptical of it.

The coffin references we see toward the end of *Rabbit Is Rich* does not necessarily mean death, but it could be read a metaphor describing Harry's new found peace rooted in humanism. Updike's protagonist is now a humanist, and his humanism is the focus of the final Rabbit novel, *Rabbit At Rest*, where Rabbit finds his earthly center in Florida. He has found redemption.

Uncharacteristically, the beginning of the fourth novel, *Rabbit At Rest,* in the Rabbit series lacks the pessimistic/apocalyptic vision of humanity found in the other three novels. The only pessimistic narration remotely similar to the other novels is found on the first page, while Harry is waiting for his son's arrival at the Florida airport, " … Rabbit Angstrom has a funny sudden feeling that what he has come to meet, what's floating in unseen about to land, is not his son Nelson and daughter-in-law Pru and their two children but something ominous and intimately his: his own death shaped vaguely like an airplane (*Rabbit At Rest*, 3). Here, Rabbit appears not to be overly worried or concerned; he just "has a funny sudden feeling." The reference to Rabbit's death in the passage is not his physical death, but the death of his old way of life, and the airplane carries with it the mechanisms, daughter-in-law Pru and his son Nelson, to bring about that death and usher in a more peaceful existence. The airplane is seen as a technological device that destroys people through collisions and mechanical failures.

Updike immediately informs the reader that Harry has found his earthly center or peaceful existence in Florida, "He is innocently proud that she [Janice] looks ... like these other American grandmothers who can afford to be here in this land of constant sunshine and eternal youth" (*Rabbit At Rest*, 5). Here, Rabbit no longer lives in darkness and despair as in *Rabbit Redux*, "...Pine street at this hour is dark ... " (*Rabbit At Rest*, 13). He now lives in the Florida sunlight. Rabbit also is indifferent about money. In *Rabbit At Rest* "Janice is Rich;" whereas, in the third novel, "*Rabbit Is Rich.*" Money, for Rabbit, was the symbol of power, a technology to be used, but now he no longer cares about it—he only wants to be comfortable. He has humanistic concerns. Another indication of Harry's discovered earthly center is found when the tables are turned on him by the other people in the Florida retirement community. As pointed out in Chapters one and two, Harry studied people as if they were under a microscope, but now he is being studied by the condo residents, "In their condo building in fact he and Janice are pets of a sort, being gentiles: they're considered cute" (*Rabbit At Rest*, 6).

Right before Nelson's airplane is to arrive, Harry begins to think of recent airplane crashes and outer space, " ...with a roar and giant ripping noise and scattered screams this whole cozy world dropping away and nothing under you but black space and your chest squeezed by the terrible unbreathable cold ... with the merciless chill of death from outer space still in them (*Rabbit At Rest*, 8-9). Here, the narrator offers a different perspective on space different from those presented in the previous novels. Rabbit is concerned about his fellow humans and how space squeezes their chest and forces into them "the merciless chill of death." This foreboding narration is present up to the point when the plane finally lands.

When Harry greets his son and the grandchildren, a tenderness to Rabbit's nature is shown, "With a shrug of exasperation Harry gives up and leans in close and kisses Roy's velvety cheek, finer than velvet, still, feverish with sleep and shakes his own son's small and clammy hand" (*Rabbit At Rest*, 12). In the first two novels, very few soft and sympathetic narrations were associated with Rabbit because he was always studying humanity, but in the final novel several are present, indicating further change in Rabbit's character as he further embraces his humanistic impulses and desires. Pru reinforces Rabbit's change by saying "The sunny South agrees with you" (*Rabbit At Rest*, 14). One such change is shown in Rabbit's ability to want to cry. As the Angstroms walk to the parking lot to drive back home, Harry and his granddaughter Judy become separated from the others. They walk around the parking until they find the car and decide to wait for the others. Judy is tired and frightened, and Harry sits down beside her, thinking, "He too wouldn't mind having a cry ..." (*Rabbit At Rest*, 23).

After everyone has settled into Harry's home and sleeping quarters have been determined, Rabbit lies in bed thinking of the five winters he has lived in Florida and the history of Deleon, Florida and the South. The narrator reveals that Harry has now taken up reading history books, the story of humanity, as a hobby (*Rabbit At Rest*, 44). He is no longer studying space. This is a new and interesting dimension to Rabbit. In contrast, in *Rabbit Redux* he would listen to the news to learn about the Apollo 11 mission, and in *Rabbit Is Rich* he read *Consumer Reports* and scanned the newspapers for the latest information on outer space. Perhaps Harry's new interest in history further illustrates his humanistic qualities. Now, he is interested in the accomplishments of men and women and not the technological achievements people have given to the world. This suggests that there is hope for keeping technology in its proper perspective. The following morning he suggests to his grandchildren—after they were disappointed about not seeing Disney—possible places they can visit. One of the places is the Edison House, which is frowned upon by the children, "Maybe the invention of the telephone and the phonograph doesn't seem too exciting to kids raised on all this computerized crap they have now," Rabbit says (*Rabbit At Rest*, 50). Here, Harry is being openly critical of postmodern technology. Technology is its own stature by focusing upon itself. Who can recall the inventor of the cellular phone? Yet, everyone knows of the technology. The human equation is gone. The Church must restore it.

Another example of Rabbit's rejection of technology is described during a golf game following breakfast. In *Rabbit Is Rich* Harry would think about the scientific side to golf: the arc and speed of the swing must be just right. But now he ignores what the magazines' advise. He thinks "So, in golf, the distances, the hundreds of yards, dissolve to a few effortless swings if you find the inner magic, the key" (*Rabbit At Rest*, 56). The important words here are "inner magic" because instead of relying on science to improve his game he now looks inward for answers taking on a spiritual and humanistic dimension to his character. Before moving to Florida, he looked outward or toward new Archimedean points, such as the affair with Ruth and the Jill and Skeeter incident, to find answers and change himself, but he now realizes the answers to all his questions are in his own heart. After the golf game, Harry and his golfing party are in the clubhouse talking. One of the men suggests that Harry should visit an old car museum because Rabbit once sold cars, but Harry gives a surprising response, " ...I sell'em, but I've never really understood the damn things. To me they're all alike. Great if they go, lousy if they don't" (*Rabbit At Rest*, 72). This is a clear change in attitude. In *Rabbit Is Rich* he wanted to kill his son for scratching his car, but now he is indifferent to cars. They have lost their importance to him, showing that he is longer manipulated by technology. Rabbit is free. Humanity desires freedom, but people think technology creates freedom. This is an illusion. Following the clubhouse scene, a tired Rabbit goes home to take a rest. The narrator says, "[he wanted to] ... close his eyes on the sound of the bird dryly chirping in the Norfolk pine, and succumb to the great heaviness of being" (*Rabbit At Rest*, 76). Again, Updike associates a tender scene with Rabbit to show how he is responsive to the world around him. While Rabbit is sleeping, he has a dream about space, "The space he was dreaming of he now recognizes as his rib cage, as if he has become his own heart, a huffing puffing pumping man at mid-court, waiting for the whistle and the high-reaching jump off (*Rabbit At Rest*, 78). He has turned inward, and when all is said and done for Rabbit and really all for men and women, self-realization and self-actualization are what's important. Rabbit perceives he was wrong to look externally to find peace. He now understands that during his high school days he held the key—found within his rib cage or his heart—that would unlock inner-peace or final rest. The answer to discovering his lost humanity was obscured by a postmodern, technological world, leaving Rabbit confused and running scared. Four pages after the dream sequence, Janice informed her husband that the days of her father were easier, "That was a simpler world" (*Rabbit At Rest,* 83).

Shortly after Harry wakes up from his dream, the Angstroms, except for Nelson who is out looking for drugs to satisfy his cocaine dependency, go to a restaurant. Nelson never shows up for dinner. Harry senses that his son is lost in a void similar to that he encountered with Thelma. He approached that void and came back a changed man, but he knows Nelson is having difficulties returning or coming back home from his own void to his earthly center, "Harry ... looks up at the teeming sky and thinks, there is no mercy. The stark plummy stars press down and the depth of the galactic void for an instant makes you feel suspended upside down (*Rabbit At Rest,* 85). Here, the language is different than what was found in the previous novels that discussed the void. Before, Harry found himself in the void and darkness that was all around him, but now the narrator says the void "makes you feel suspended," indicating a sort of warning about the direction science is taking humanity or a description of what a person feels when inside the void; Nelson is now in that void. His father's void was his desire to move and constantly change his world; Nelson's void is drug abuse.

The next significant scene occurs when Harry and Janice take the grandchildren to various historical points of interest. The first place they tour is the Edison House. After the tour Harry says, "I was interested ... in all those failures he had in developing the storage battery. You wouldn't think it would be so tough. How many—nine thousand experiments?" (*Rabbit At Rest,* 98). Harry is interested in the imperfect nature of humanity and how that imperfection makes us who we are. Through genetic selection those flaws that make us who we are will one day eliminate humanity as we know it in favor of a homogenized gathering of people. Rabbit finds this interesting based upon his newly discovered Self. Even at the heart of scientific advancement beats the human story, a story of failure and success, trial and error. Harry now realizes that all of us are only human--born to make mistakes. The four Angstroms then go to another location, Mirror Lake, to observe the Flamingo Lagoon. Adhering to the true humanistic notion of humanity's movement away from God, Updike writes "Do you still believe in God, if people keep telling you you are God?" (*Rabbit At Rest*, 103). As they observe the birds, " …they stand marveling, the four human beings, as if the space between far-flung planets has been abolished, so different do these living things loom from themselves. The earth is many planets, that intersect only at moments" (*Rabbit At Rest*, 103). Here, the universe is not scientifically structured or formalistic. The narration is humanistic because there are no longer planets in the universe or a void, but "The earth is many planets" and man's place is on the earth being a part of the world around him.

After the day of touring, the children are badgering Harry because he accidentally ate bird food, thinking it was some sort of snack food. Janice tries to comfort her husband by saying it was a "natural mistake," and Harry responds "'That's the kind I make,' he says. 'Natural ones'" (*Rabbit At Rest*, 105). Rabbit no longer makes "scientific mistakes," such as treating people as objects to be studied; he now makes "Natural ones." Again, our "natural mistakes" make us who we are.

Throughout much of the Rabbit series, many allusions to death are scattered in the text, but in the final novel the reader sees, instead, many images of birth and rebirth—metaphors that continue portraying Updike's protagonist as a changed person. Rabbit tells Roy that the "Cruelest thing people do is fish." Here, Rabbit openly expresses his concern for nature or the world around him. At one time he treated people cruelly and objectified them. Then, the newscaster reports that "'An adult manatee with calf was reported'" (*Rabbit At Rest*, 110), symbolizing birth and the hope of a future. This idea of birth contradicts the title, if the title is to be read as death. After the news and late night television, Rabbit reflects on the day with Janice, "Today, he says. In that crowd going through the Edison place. Did I look as though I fit in?" (*Rabbit At Rest*, 115) Most of Harry's life was spent running from humanity. Now, he is asking Janice if he fits in with humanity, or he wants to know if he is now a part of it.

The next day Rabbit takes Judy sail boating—the act that brings on his first major heart attack. As the two go skimming across the ocean, Updike writes "'Centerboard down,' he (Rabbit) commands, a captain at last, at the mere age of fifty-five" (*Rabbit At Rest,* 127). The acknowledgment that Harry is now a captain suggests he is in control of his own life. Unfortunately, he is not because the boat turns over, and Rabbit is forced to save his granddaughter, despite experiencing the beginnings of a heart attack. He fights to get the boat upwards, and the two work to climb onto the craft. Harry struggles to get the boat back to shore—a reminder of the struggle he underwent throughout much of his life. He safely lands on the shore and drops to the sand with a heart attack. Meanwhile, Janice and Nelson are back at the condo discussing Nelson's drug problem. Janice is explaining to her son why Harry acts the way he does, "He had a hard time when we were younger giving up his dreams and his freedom but he seems to be at peace now" (*Rabbit At Rest,* 145). Janice's admission that Harry had it rough when he was younger verifies that her husband was confused, but she also says "he seems to be at peace now," which clearly states she thinks Rabbit has changed. Humanity, faith, and science, too, can change.

Soon after the heart attack Rabbit is rushed to the hospital, and Janice is notified of her husband's condition by Pru. After everyone has visited Harry and left, Janice chooses not to stay with her husband. She appears to be extremely cold—as if she has taken on the uncaring personality Rabbit had as a young man—by leaving a sick Rabbit in the hospital to attend an origami demonstration (*Rabbit At Rest,* 171). She now becomes *Everywoman.* While Rabbit is lying in the hospital bed, he begins to question his newly discovered humanism, "He has something evil and weak inside him that might betray him at any minute into that icy blackness Bernie talked about" (*Rabbit At Rest,* 174). He begins to realize but not understand the "scientific" impulse he carried throughout his adult life, and this frightens him because he has been to that "ice blackness" and does not want to go back.

Chapter 2 begins with Harry and Janice returning to their Mount Judge home for the spring and summer. The chapter begins, similar to the beginning of a passage in *Rabbit, Run* (*Rabbit, Run* 127), with "Sun and moon, rise and fall" (*Rabbit At Rest,* 181), indicating changing or phases of life. Because the first chapter ended with Rabbit having a massive heart attack, one would think the second chapter would begin with images of death to remain consistent with the title, but the opening narration is quite the contrary. Updike describes the blossoming of spring, i.e. rebirth, and the magnolias and quince are in bloom and "a red haze of budding fills the maples" (*Rabbit At Rest*, 181). The phases of the sun and moon, along with the description of spring or rebirth, indicate that Rabbit has survived the first test of his humanity, being left by Janice in the hospital while confronting his own mortality, so he now can continue growing like the newly opened maples, " …Rabbit likes to drive around, freshening his memory and hurting himself with the pieces of his old self that cling to almost every corner of the Brewer area" (*Rabbit At Rest*, 181). Here, Harry realizes that by confronting his painful past he can overcome his fears of slipping back to that way of life. He can stay clear of the void.

But, can humanity stay clear of the void? Updike wrestles with this question. Rabbit begins exercising/jogging again, and while he is running, he thinks. "And those running tights the young women wear now, so they look like spacewomen, raspberry red and electric green so tight they show every muscle right into the crack between the buttocks, what is the point then? Display. Young animals need to display" (*Rabbit At Rest*, 184). He continues, "We're turning into mad dogs—the human race is one big swamp of viruses" (*Rabbit At Rest*, 185). By using the term "viruses," the narrator is suggesting that something needs to be remedied. Janice sums up the theme of Chapter 2, while the two are out driving around. Rabbit tells Janice he does not remember "these trees" being planted in downtown Brewer. Janice responds "'You've seen, it's just you see differently now'" (*Rabbit At Rest*, 188). This statement clearly shows Rabbit does in fact see the world in a different light now.

After two weeks in Mount Judge, Harry decides to visit Thelma, the woman with whom he had an affair for several years. Harry wants to believe he had the affair only for sex, but now he realizes he loved her like he loves all of humanity now. Thelma tells him that he is not the center of the universe, but Rabbit, being a representative of humanity, knows he is. When he first had sex with Thelma, the center of the universe was the inevitable void, "Black box of nothingness, is what it felt like with Thelma" (*Rabbit At Rest*, 219). Thelma reminds Harry of the void he once experienced, which is why love does not happen between the two former lovers, and they basically stay separated. Harry has grown and developed into a new man with humanistic concerns; thus, he is concerned with people and their feelings.

Much of the second chapter focuses on something rotten with humanity. Humanity is corrupted, and its core has become diseased and distant and cold. In this chapter, Rabbit meets with his old friend Charlie Stavros [with whom his wife Janice had an affair] because he suspects something is wrong with the financial situation at the lot, a metaphor for humanity. They talk about the world and about women, "These women seem visitors from a slimmed-down future where sex is just another exercise and we all live in sealed cubicles and communicate through computers" (*Rabbit At Rest*, 231). This was written before the age of text messaging and emailing. We have traded face-to-face dialogue for digital information sent through cyber space. The danger with emails or text messaging is the inability to read facial expressions and mannerisms. A great part communicating is nonverbal. That is what makes us human. Technology de-humanizes us by eliminating parts of how we communicate with one another—face to face contact is disappearing. Conflicts are handled by emails rather than direct confrontation. Updike is the seer or prophet of the Old Testament delivering his message on the state of the human race and where it is headed if it does not change course. He sees the future as a place where intimacy is gone, and everyone lives in isolation. Updike continues with this criticism of the technological world, "We are each of us like our little blue planet, hung in black space, upheld by nothing but our mutual reassurances, our loving lies" (*Rabbit At Rest*, 264). In other words, humanity is headed in the same direction where Rabbit once was, resulting in a kind of isolation similar to that of the infinite darkness of space, where science dares to tread. Updike is not calling for an end to technology. He offers a warning to science to keep the human aspect of technology in consideration. Similarly, the Church must take on the same responsibility.

Harry decides to confront his accountant Lyle at the lot about the financial situation of the lot. The two are in conflict because Lyle is a homosexual dying of AIDS, and he is hiding something from Rabbit. Later, before Harry goes into the hospital for an examination and decides on an angioplasty, he tells Janice about Lyle's refusal to let him see the books, and that she is the only one who can get them. Rabbit dislikes homosexuals not because of who they are but what they do, "Bottoms. Thelma. That casket of nothingness. Probing the void" (*Rabbit At Rest,* 281). He does not want to see anyone enter that void, and he fears the void as should all people.

Harry enters the hospital once again to have his arteries cleared, and once again Janice leaves her husband in the hospital, so she can go to her Realtors class. The clearing of his arteries is a metaphor for removing the hidden remaining "scientific" impulses left in Rabbit's heart. People must go through a cleansing from technology in order to appreciate community. He gets out of the hospital, and Rabbit no longer runs; instead, he walks for exercise and sees a brighter, clearer Brewer or a better life. The more he returns to humanity the better his life becomes. He once saw Brewer as dull and gritty (*Rabbit At Rest,* 326). The narrator now says "We're using it all up. Harry thinks. The world" (*Rabbit At Rest,* 327). At the end of Chapter 2, Rabbit sleeps with his daughter-in-law Pru.

Rabbit's sexual encounter with Pru is an act of love. All the other sex scenes from *Rabbit, Run* to *Rabbit Is Rich* describe sex in vulgar and crude terminology. In *Rabbit, Run* he makes Ruth perform oral sex, and he rubs his penis against Janice's buttocks for selfish, sexual pleasure after her birthing of Nelson. In *Rabbit Redux,* he uses profanity to describe his sexual relations with an eighteen-year-old girl, and he watches Skeeter sexually abuse her. In *Rabbit Is Rich,* Harry and Thelma have sex, and he, then, defiles Thelma by urinating on her—the way we are defiling one another. However, in this last novel, *Rabbit At Rest,* the encounter with Pru is different. Pru seduces him, and the scene is tenderly described. Pru runs her finger gently down Harry's chest and the two softly kiss and embrace (*Rabbit At Rest,* 345). While this is happening, the wind and rain whip outside the window, bringing a mythological or Romantic element to the scene (*Rabbit At Rest,* 346). Crude language serves an important function for tracing Rabbit's development.

Chapter 3 begins with Harry increasing his financial investigation of Nelson's operations of the car lot, and he is forced to manage it once again because Nelson is in a drug rehabilitation center. He talks with Elvira, one of the sales crew on the lot. She says "You matter to everybody, Harry, if that's what you're hinting at" (*Rabbit At Rest,* 358). This reaffirms the significance of Rabbit's existence in the world. Science does not validate or affirm one's essence or existence beyond the physiological. That is its shortcoming. Church can provide that validation.

Rabbit is talked into playing Uncle Sam in the town's parade. The only significance of this scene is what Janice tells him about wearing the wig, "It's not insulting, it's interesting. I never saw your feminine side before" (*Rabbit At Rest,* 363). Now, Harry is truly in touch with all of humanity: men and women. While he is walking in the parade, Harry expresses concern for the world, "The greenhouse effect, he thinks. The hole in the ozone. When the ice in Antarctica goes, we'll all be drowned" (*Rabbit At Rest,* 370-371). He later learns that Thelma dies from her Lupus. Rabbit could not think this way until he got in touch with his human side. Science can provide the facts and causes of global warming and predict what will happen as well as develop tools to tackle the problem, but it takes humanity working together, using those tools, to actually stop it.

After Thelma's funeral service, Rabbit starts discussions about returning to Florida. He learns that his wife does not want to go back; she wants to stay and start a realty business. Also, Rabbit and Thelma's husband Ronnie play golf together and carry on a long discussion over the merits of Voyager Two (*Rabbit At Rest,* 411-413), reminiscent of *Rabbit Redux.* But the discussion ends on a critical note of space travel, "The image faintly sickens Harry, of Voyager taking those last shots of Neptune and then sailing off into the void, forever. How can you believe how much void there is?" (*Rabbit At Rest,* 413). Clearly, Rabbit no longer glorifies space travel. He sees it as a destructive influence on the human race.

Soon after Rabbit's rejection of space travel, Pru admits to having an affair with her father in law. Rabbit, who sees his sexual encounter with Pru as an expression of love, now realizes that he must leave Pennsylvania and return to the land where he found rest, "The spaceship is upon him, with all its rivets and blinking lights" (*Rabbit At Rest,* 432). Here, Rabbit is not identifying with as previously the "spaceship," but the spaceship is perceived as a threat to Rabbit, crushing down upon him from outer space as if seeking revenge for Rabbit's denial of space exploration. Now, instead of Rabbit using space as a way to escape humanity, space is now coming down on him, forcing him to pack his bags and return to Deleon, Florida.

About midway through his drive back to Florida, he stops at a hotel and calls his family. Pru answers the telephone, and asks the most important question in the novel, "'Where on earth are you?'" (*Rabbit At Rest,* 444). He responds "'Far away, where everybody wants me'" (*Rabbit At Rest,* 444). His response is not to be taken in a negative manner because everyone knows—indicate by all the references to how the South agrees with him—that Florida is where he is most comfortable because according to the narrator "Tomorrow [when he arrives in Florida], life will find him again" (*Rabbit At Rest,* 457).

Once in Florida he begins to worry about himself and others. Rabbit is concerned about what he did to Nelson by making love to Pru. He also worries about Janice not calling him. He wonders if Janice has been in some kind of accident (*Rabbit At Rest,* 469). Rabbit begins to start taking better care of himself. Updike writes, "He prolongs his walks, feeling stronger, more comfortable in this strange city ..." (*Rabbit At Rest,* 479). He starts reading history books again, or studying the accomplishments of humanity, and he is eliminating fat from his diet—every indication that he is getting healthier and not approaching death. When his scientist nature dominated his actions, Rabbit was dying. Now, he cares for people and the world. It is his getting in touch with his impulse to be a part of humanity that gave him "life." Being human is multi-faceted. We are not all science or all humanism or all religion. All these come together to define who we are, but when one is not kept in balance, humanity heads down a treacherous road.

During Rabbit's walks, he stops in the poor side of town to watch the boys play basketball, "Rabbit is happy to think that the world isn't yet too crowded to have a few of these underused pockets left" (*Rabbit At Rest,* 487). This narration contradicts the opening page of *Rabbit, Run* when he plays street basketball with some Brewer boys, "The kids keep coming, they keep crowding you up" (*Rabbit, Run,* 9). Rabbit now sees the world differently. As a young man, he felt there was no place for him, so he metaphorically looked to the stars to find his place in the universe; Rabbit represents modernity's attempt to find himself in the technological age. Science seems to provide all the answers from the

Big Band to the gene that explains altruism. Rabbit makes his mark on the world not by conquering space through his shifting Archimedean point which will only lead to destruction, but rather, by embracing humanity. Rabbit challenges one of the boys to a basketball game. He pushes himself too hard and has another heart attack, leaving him in the hospital's intensive care unit. The family rushes to Florida to see him. Janice and Nelson forgive Rabbit because they finally realize how important he was in their lives, i.e. for humanity. He helped Janice become independent and successful, and he helped Nelson get off the drugs by forcing or pressing his son to take a hard look at his life. He also helped Pru realize that she is a woman who counts in the world and is not just Nelson's wife. Only the interaction of people can this be accomplished. Science cannot do it.

Robert Regan's essay, "Updike's Symbol of the Center," becomes important when read while considering *Rabbit At Rest* because Rabbit never had a center in which his experiences could radiate, leaving Harry lost in the world. Rabbit is at rest because he now has a center to experience life. It took a life time to obtain it. Throughout much of the series Rabbit—holding true to Arendt's essay—intentionally alienated himself from humanity because he saw mankind as merely organic beings to study. Now, he sees the world differently.

Many scholars believe that Rabbit died at the end of the novel. The contrary has happened: Rabbit found life. He did not die, but at near death he is closer to humanity than he was all his life. Rabbit represents humanity's struggle to find himself in an ever changing and moving technological, postmodern world. Harry is *Everyman,* one of us struggling and trying to make sense of a rapidly changing world driven by technological advancements that make the previous year obsolete. Rabbit went to the void and discovered his lost self. Rabbit is Reborn. Rabbit is not a destroyer, as stated by many critics, but in fact he is the bringer of life for revealing the importance of humanity. Rabbit had always feared making a commitment to humanity, but in the end he realizes humanity "'isn't so bad'" (*Rabbit At Rest,* 512).

In some of Updike's more recent works, this concern with the role of science and its place within the greater human picture continues to be a noteworthy topic for Updike. Take his 1997 novel, *Toward the End of Time.*

The novel is set in a period immediately following a war between China and the United States, a war that was waged with technology. Technology plays an essential role in this war with China. The United States survived the war in which society remains basically the same with the exception of a broken government and gangs roaming the streets. Despite the survival, one can sense a movement toward the end of time, but the nature of the end is not clear. Perhaps, it is the end of humanity but not the annihilation of people. This challenges Harry's newly discovered life through contact with humanity in *Rabbit At Rest*. The main character who is also narrates the story says, "The sun is a star. Christianity said God is man. Humanism said Man is God. Today the sages say, via such Jainist cosmogonies as string theory and the inflationary hypothesis, that everything is nothing. The cosmos is a free lunch, a quantum fluctuation" (*Toward the End of Time*, 34). Apparently, science did not have the last word for humanity did indeed survive. Furthermore, while the main narrator and his wife Dierdre are in church on Easter morning [note: the Church has survived the war], His mind begins to wander, "Superposition, I thought. Before Christ ascended, He was in what quantum theory calls superposition—neither here nor there, up nor down. He was Schrodinger's cat (*Toward the End of Time*, 116)." Updike enters the realm of quantum physics, where perhaps the finger prints of God can be found.

In both these quotes scientific language replaces the language of theology and humanism. The sages are no longer prophets and philosophers, but are scientists. Christ's ascension is explained in terms of quantum physics and hypotheses, and the role of humanity is diminished. This theme is continued in a rather extensive discussion on the nature of the cosmos and the place of humanity in it. Humanity is reduced from its spiritual, philosophical, and creative aspects to strictly intellectual, " ...scientists only toward the end of the last millennium formulated its primal place among the forces of creation. The particles smaller than a quark, it was reluctantly proclaimed, are purely mathematical, that is to say, mental" (*Toward the End of Time*, 151-52). In addition, evolution of intelligent life is based upon chemical and atomic laws.

However, with all this scientific explanation of the universe and the nature of humanity, the main character pronounces, "And yet I am insufficiently reassured" (*Toward the End of Time,* 152). In other words, he wants something more from life.

He intellectually accepts the scientific understanding of the universe and how it came about, i.e. Big Bang theory, but that is not enough for him. There is something more intrinsic to life not so much how it got here, but why is it here, and where does it go. What is its purpose? If there is no purpose, then, everything we do are intellectual exercises designed to preoccupy us until we die.

Updike sums up the challenge facing all people and, yes, that includes the Church of the 21ˢᵗ Century. Updike's novel *Villages* published in 2005 presents the argument in more direct language. The main character Owen is talking to a friend concerning the role and place of technology, "Ian, what's missing began to be missing a long time ago with Copernicus and Martin Luther, and you can't blame technology for not bringing it back" (*Villages,* 198). Technology is in control, but a sympathetic spin is placed upon technology and science because humanity needs scientific advancement, but it must be kept under scrutiny. Copernicus let the proverbial cat out of the bag leading to the diminishment of faith and the reduction of humanity. There is no going back. "It's the Devil's bargain, Ian—medicine and electricity and rocket science in exchange for an empty heaven" (*Villages,* 198). The "empty heaven" marks the end of religion. Owen is concerned why he became so emotionally attached to this discussion with Ian. He became angry, "[Owen] wondered why he had become so heated; he didn't want to believe this. He wanted to have technology and illusions, too: both were the same ameliorative fruits of human imagination" (*Villages,* 199). He has every reason to be angry because what is being discussed is an end to what it means to be human. This, as we have seen in the Rabbit novels, is the struggle of humanity to express itself, to cry, "I have purpose and meaning." From a theological perspective, the Church provides that meaning through real, authentic community. This reintroduction of community will keep the Church from slipping into the void of cultural irrelevancy. Science cannot create community. The Church must step forward and re-introduce community.

Finally, Updike brings this discussion of science and technology in regards to their influence upon humanity to religion, mainly the Church. The Church is under great pressure to define itself in the postmodern era. Many of these intellectual meanderings in *Villages* happen while in Church, "The church in strategic retreat abandons the cosmos to physics, and takes refuge in the personal—the cosmos of fragile, evanescent consciousness" (*Villages,* 271). This is the place of the Church. It is hidden not knowing how to be seen. As science moves forward, the relevancy of the Church will be more and more drawn into question not only Christianity but all religions when science develops ways to meet every man, woman, and child on the planet their physical needs, and to prevent disease and extend life. The "strategic retreat of the church" signifies the co-opting of religion by science. In *Villages,* the human condition is fully described, "Yet we seek to impose patterns of meaning around ourselves, interlocking networks vectored back to the ego, de point de depart, if not the Archimedean Point that lifts this heavy, tangled, cluttered world into schematic forum we can manipulate" (*Villages,* 308).

The consequences of unchecked scientific advancement is described by Updike in *Rabbit At Rest,* "...with a roar and giant ripping noise and scattered screams this whole cozy world dropping away and nothing under you but black space and your chest squeezed by the terrible and unbreathable cold ... with the merciless chill of death from outer space still in them (*Rabbit At Rest,* 8-9). And so, this is where we are. Updike does not argue for the elimination of science and technological advancement, and neither does this book. The claim posited by Updike is that unchecked science can be destructive. Forces, such as the Church, must be in place in order to balance such advancements. Advancements are good as long as science does not blindly run forward into the future with disregard for consequences. Rabbit's story is our story. We are confused, and we spend our lives trying to discover who we really are. In the postmodern world, science and technology are supposed to bring meaning and purpose, but they do not. Our souls cry out for something with purpose. The next chapter explores the role of the Church as sciences marches forward.

Chapter 3: Church and Science

… with a roar and giant ripping noise and scattered screams this whole
cozy world dropping away and nothing under you but black space and
your chest squeezed by the terrible unbreathable cold … with the merciless
chill of death from outer space still in them (Rabbit At Rest, 8-9).

In 1633, Galileo was forced by the Roman Catholic Church to refute his claim that the earth was not in fact the center of the universe. Here, the tension and conflict began. Today, science is at the forefront of postmodern society. In such a world, God is being reduced, especially in mainline Protestant churches, to the God of the gaps—the Divine is used to explain those things that are currently unexplainable, thus, filling the gaps of knowledge. However, as science progresses fewer gaps remain. What happens when science fills all the gaps, and where, then, is God? Is God really dead, as indicated by the "God-is-Dead" theology of the 1960s? *Think Tank,* a discussion program on PBS, addressed the issue of the collision between science and religion. Margaret

Wertheim, who was on the discussion panel, summed up the state of religion in a technological-driven culture, "Scientists ... are wanting to set themselves up as the new theologians." There is a power struggle, and science wants to claim more and more of the world, but what does science say about a moral code? (Wertheim Think Tank, 3). There is research now that might suggest the existence of a moral gene which keeps us from basically destroying one another. Such a gene means human behavior is deterministic in nature. British biologist William D. Hamilton in 1964 proposed an "altruistic gene." He connected this to a "kin" gene. For example, it makes more sense for a chimpanzee to share food with a sibling than to give food to an unrelated chimp. This helps ensure that his family genes are brought forward (Wright, 160-61). It is all about advancing one's genetic material. There is no love for love's sake. It is all about preserving and moving forward one's genes over another's genes.

Opposition between science and religion or faith does not necessarily mean annihilation. World class athletes perform best when their opponent is equally competitive. They compete against each other and shake hands after the race. Caterpillars becoming butterflies must push and struggle their way through their cocoons in order to develop their wings for flight. If they do not struggle, the wings do not develop, and hence, they die. The great creeds and doctrines of the Church arose out of its conflict with Gnosticism, Arianism, Marcion, and so on. All these groups were deemed heretical; thus, direct conflict forced the fledgling Christian movement to define who they were amidst Jewish and other competing groups, such as Gnosticism. Gnosticism believes in the duality of the universe—the world/flesh is evil and the spirit is good. There is a divine spark trapped in us, and it must be released from the prison of the flesh. They believed the world was evil; this is why the Apostles' Creed says, "I believe in God the Father, *maker of heaven and earth ...* " [emphasis mine]. If God made the earth, then, it must be good, for God so loved the world. Conflict can be good. Conflict does not necessarily mean destruction. Arianism denied the true Divinity of Jesus the Christ. They believed Jesus was created by God from nothing to be an instrument for the creation of the world. However, the Apostles' Creed maintains that the faithful believe "in Jesus Christ His only *begotten Son ...* [emphasis mine]." Here, Jesus is begotten not made. The Nicene Creed is even more specific, "We believe in one Lord, Jesus Christ, the only Son of God, eternally *begotten of the Father, God from God, true God from true God, begotten not made, of one being with the Father* ... [emphasis mine]." And Marcion believed there was a separation between the Old Testament and the New Testament to the extent that Marcion believed there were two gods, the god of vengeance and judgment (Old Testament) and the god of love (New Testament). The creator god had nothing to do with the loving god of the New Testament. The Nicene Creed addresses Marcion by stating, "We believe in *one God, the Father, the Almighty, maker of heaven and earth, of all that is, seen and unseen* [emphasis mine]."

Thus, conflict is good because it forges belief. For the early Church, conflict provided a set of doctrines to help people understand their faith. In the face of opposition, it is important for people to know what they believe in order to hold firm when conflict arises, and by holding firm, one's faith becomes stronger, "But as for you, teach what is consistent with sound doctrine" (Titus 2:1). Obviously, the doctrine that came out of those early struggles must have been sound because they are with us to this day. The problem with the Church today is that its conflict is misplaced or misguided. Theological differences are not the battlegrounds within the body of the Church. Unrestricted, technological achievements and advancements pose the greatest threat to Christianity and religion in general. Baptists, Methodists, Presbyterians, Pentecostals, Lutherans and Church of Christ, Liberals and Conservatives, and Protestants and Roman Catholics should not be in conflict with each other—"Now I appeal to you, brothers and sisters, by the name of our Lord Jesus Christ, that all of you be in agreement and that there be no divisions among you, but that you be united in the same mind and the same purpose" (1 Corinthians 1:10), but rather view one another as different parts of the body of Christ, the Church, "For just as the body is one and has many members, and all the members of the body, though many, are one body, so it is with Christ. For in the one spirit we were all baptized into one body—Jews or Greeks, slaves or free—and we were all made to drink of one Spirit" (1 Corinthians 12:12-13). Churches are splitting, arguing, and condemning each other. Furthermore, doctrine, creeds, and/or reaffirmation of belief and faith are not happening amidst these denominational conflicts including liberal verses conservative oppositions. Nothing constructive is coming out of the liberal-verses-conservative attacks unlike the Early Church which addressed other Christian groups that were significantly different in their doctrines. Conflict and opposition within the body of Christ in the 21st century accomplishes nothing. Denominational squabbles hurt the Church in the long term because today, more than ever, people have several secular choices before them, so why choose to belong to a group that cannot get along with each other. The Church, unlike science which builds upon previous knowledge, tends not to add to the theological building blocks laid down in the early years of the Church. Instead, the Church tends to fragment or splinter, but the various body parts of the Church must find commonality through such ancient doctrines as the Holy Trinity; and then, build upon standard, historical Christianity in order to make it relevant for the 21st century. This includes adapting fourth century theological language into 21st century thought. Instead, the misguided conflicts within the Church are tearing it down. Stop fighting over baptism and start fighting the practice of cloning by asking science, "How far are you willing to take cloning?" When churches take such a unified approach, this does not mean surrendering each church's distinctive theological and ideological identity, but differences must be set aside or the Church runs the risk of irrelevancy to a generation with institutional mistrust and cyber communities.

The Church in order to define itself, to set itself apart, in this scientific age must fight relevant battles with science and within the context of our technological-driven culture. At this point of conflict Church discovers and defines itself and its role in and for the 21st century. This conflict need not be aggressive or ill-tempered. It can be an amiable conflict in which both parties (science/technology and Church) benefit from the dialogue and hopefully grow and move forward through the ages.

The Church's *sacra doctrina* must assert itself to be the judge of the sciences, which inevitably crosses over into the moral and ethical realms where the Church should directly engage science in an amiable fashion by raising the questions: How will humanity benefit by this? And what are the potential dangers? How will this affect the stature of humanity? Thus, if the Church does not carry out this task, then, who will?

According to theologian and ethicist Stanley Hauerwas, the validation of science and philosophy does not depend on our knowledge of God; also, Aquinas did not consider the relationship between theology and the other sciences in that way. In his book, *With the Grain of the Universe*, Hauerwas extensively quotes Aquinas from his *Summa Theological 1.6.2,*

> *The principles of other sciences either are evident and cannot be proved, or are proved by natural reason through some other science. But the knowledge proper to this science comes through revelation, and not through natural reason. Therefore it has no concern to prove the principles of the other sciences, but only to judge them.* [This is an essential role of the Church in the postmodern world.] *Whatsoever is found in other sciences contrary to any truth of this science, must be condemned as false: "Destroying counsels and every height that exalted itself against the knowledge of God" (2 Corinthians 10:4-5)* (Hauerwas 23-24).

What Aquinas puts forward is that science has a legitimate place in the world. It serves its purpose, and it is not up to theology to disprove or prove the sciences. However, it is essential for the Church to judge the sciences and technologies as either lifting up humanity or degrading humanity.

Francis S. Collins in his book, *The Language of God,* tries to accommodate science and religion from the scientific perspective rather than a religious one. He uses miracles as a discussion point, and in this discussion he cites the Scottish theologian The Reverend Thomas Bayes' theorem for observing a particular event and the explanation for that event. This theorem is useful, according to Collins, when one is faced with two possible explanations for one event, such as the parting of the Red Sea. Despite being developed by a theologian, Bayes' Theorem applies mathematics and scientific analysis to determine the veracity of miracles (Collins, 49). Ultimately, the truth of a miracle—did it happen or not—gets reduced to probabilities and likelihoods. Collins misses the greater picture here. The sole purpose of miracles in the

Bible is to point beyond themselves to the kingdom of God rather than focusing on a particular event, such as Jesus healing the blind man. The healing was not so much about the man being able to see again, but the purpose of the healing was to say, "This is what the kingdom of God is to be." Take a cancer patient who is suddenly cured. Is it a miracle? Or, did something happen physiologically to bring about the healing? From a Biblical perspective, if the disappearance of the patient's cancer in some way points to the Kingdom of God, then, it is a miracle. How it happened is irrelevant. Postmodern people struggle more with what it means to be human in the universe because the universe is much larger than it was at any time before. People are searching for relevance and significance, so how the world was created is unimportant to many.

Collins acknowledges that the probability for miracles to happen is low, but they can happen. "Whatever the personal view, it is crucial that a healthy skepticism be applied when interpreting potentially miraculous events, lest the integrity and rationality of the religious perspective be brought into question" (Collins, 51).

In his book, *Jesus Christ for Today's World*, theologian Jurgen Moltmann saw a great need for the Church to be directly involved in our scientific world. He said salvation has been reduced to simply the salvation of the soul, or to authenticate human-centered existence. Whether consciously or unconsciously, this reduces salvation to that of the individual, the Church essentially abandoned nature or the physical world to disastrous exploitation by human beings. Instead, what is needed is the understanding of a cosmic Christ, the Messiah for the entire universe or as the apostle Paul writes, "For the creation waits with eager longing for the revealing of the children of God; for the creation was subjected to futility, not of its own will, but by the will of the one who subjected it, in hope that the creation itself will be set free from its bondage to decay and will obtain the freedom of the glory of the children of God. We know that the whole creation has been groaning in labor pains until now" (Romans 8:19-23). A cosmic Christology forces the Church to confront all aspects of existence, including science and technology. Moltmann cites the Chernobyl Nuclear facility disaster as an example of a cosmic Christology relevant to the needs of humanity. 8,000 to 10,000 people were killed at Chernobyl, and 50,000 were fatally contaminated. Chernobyl's children were born with birth defects, and remember, the half-life of plutonium is 24,000 years. Where is Christ after Chernobyl? Or, where is Christ in science? Such questions pertain to the Church's relevancy. Hence, there needs to be a return to the notion of a cosmic Christ that redeems all of creation rather than just individuals (Moltmann, 88-90). This sense of redemption truly has worldwide implications. It is radical. It challenges the status quo from societal norms to political power.

It is imperative for the Church to return to a cosmic vision of Christ acting in the world, "In that renewal there is no longer Greek and Jew, circumcised or uncircumcised, barbarian, Scythian, slave and free; but Christ is all and in all!" (Colossians 3:11). A failure of the early church was to ignore Paul's notion of Christ being all and in all. This led to a separation between grace and nature and in turn contempt for nature was born. This, according to Moltmann, had "fateful consequences, leading first to the postmodern subjugation of nature and then, in our own way, to its destruction" (Moltmann, 90). This dualism between nature and grace—made more apparent during the Enlightenment— was best articulated by Joseph Sittler who addressed the World Council of Churches in New Delhi in 1961, "The man of Enlightenment could penetrate the realm of nature, and to all intents and purposes take it as his sphere of sovereignty, because grace had either ignored this sector or rejected it. And with every new conquest of nature a piece of God died; the sphere of grace diminished to the degree in which structures and processes in nature were claimed by the now autonomous human being ... Men strut blasphemously about this wounded and threatened world as if it were their own property" (Moltmann, 90). Moltmann adds to this, "We are therefore living in a moment of crisis, a particular moment or *kairos* in which Christ and chaos meet, and we must confront the threat to nature with a 'christology of nature,' in which the power of redemption does not stop short at the hearts of men and women and their souls, but gathers in nature as a whole" (Moltmann, 90). It is interesting that Moltmann used the word "chaos" as confronting Christ. The argument goes like this: when human beings separated grace from nature it opened the door for abuses and chaos enters the picture. There needs to be a reclaiming of Paul's cosmic understanding of Christ as well as a movement away from understanding Christ solely from a personal salvation perspective which is needed to confront the threats of the postmodern age.

Creation once stood as an enclosed system without outside influence; then, humanity was added to that system making it more complex followed by the serpent, which is one of the symbols of chaos who introduces the possibility for chaos into this perfect system. Adam and Eve exercise their God-given free will, and thus, we have chaos or sin let loose in the world never knowing when it will be made known, such is the plight of humanity. Now, because of chaos, a curse was placed upon Creation. Now, Creation is vulnerable to chaos and its future unknown but known by God.

Genesis 3:17-18 states that God tells Adam, "Because … you ate from the tree which I had forbidden you to eat, cursed be the soil because of you! … It will yield you thorns and thistles, as you eat the produce of the land." Here, we see the introduction of chaos into agriculture. Farmers cannot predict when the growing season will have ample rain or not, or if it will be a cool or hot summer, or how many thorns and thistles will sprout in the soy bean field, and the same can be said for animal populations.

Paul probably had Genesis 3 in mind when he wrote Romans 8:19 through 25. It was a common belief among Paul's Jewish peers that Adam disobeyed God's command and subsequently fell into captivity to sin as well as the entire natural universe. Not only did men and women feel the pain of sin or chaos first hand, but all of all things suffered and stands in the need of redemption, or the elimination of chaos. And what is redemption? For nature, it is a return to that state of perfection prior to Adam's guilt, a time when chaos was not present.

Nature is restlessly waiting for fulfillment and meaning and completion. Creation longs to once again be unified, for Paul writes "We know that the whole creation has been groaning in labor pains until now; and not only the creation, but we ourselves groan …" (Romans 8:22). Nature is isolated from that perfect relationship with God and humans, and it finds itself in an unpredictable universe. Out of nature's loneliness it groans and moans, the wind wails; the seas sigh. In regards to the evolution-creation debate, people of faith should be more concerned with Creation's longing and less concerned with the act of creation itself. Part of this groaning and waiting involves ecological and environmental disaster.

Paul tells us we already have the first fruits or the first installment of the Spirit that came at Pentecost, and now we are waiting for the redemption of our bodies; or in other words, that last installment of the Spirit which makes us as well as the cosmos complete and whole. Chaos/Sin is no longer; thus, no illness, suffering, or pain. Pentecost was another act of Creation pushing the universe toward perfection and completion, "And suddenly from heaven there came sound like the rush of a violent wind, and it filled the entire house where they were sitting. Divided tongues, as of fire, appeared among them, and a tongue rested on each of them. ... And as this sound the crowd gathered and was bewildered, because each one heard them speaking in the native language of each" (Acts 2:1-8). In other words, we see God bringing order to chaos—a chaotic, multitude of different languages suddenly become one.

The general idea Paul is communicating is that since we have hope through the first fruits or first installment of the Spirit at Pentecost, we come to expect that something far greater than anything we have ever known is waiting for us. And like nature, we too groan inwardly and wait for that restoration. The Second Letter of Peter tells us to wait patiently for this restored relationship, a new heaven and a new earth, for it is there where righteousness shall dwell, a perfect state without chaos. There is only Divine order.

The single most destructive force faced by the Church comes from within the Church—the Creationist vs. Evolution debate. This is a no win debate for the Church, and it serves as a distraction. There are sincere people of faith who interpret Genesis 1 and 2 as literal which is inconsistent with our knowledge of the universe's age. St. Augustine, according to Christian geneticist Francis Collins, stated that it is difficult to understand what is being described in Genesis. Augustine believed Genesis should not be interpreted as if reading a science book. "It was intended as a description of who God was, who we are, and what our relationship is supposed to be with God. Augustine explicitly warns against a very narrow perspective that will put our faith at risk of looking ridiculous" (Biema, 53-54). Yet, groups insist on biblical literalism. A pro-Creationist group that founded the $27 million Creation Museum in Kentucky has started an online technical journal for the publishing of articles and studies supporting biblical views of creation. In addition, a group, like "Answers in Genesis" who perpetuate a debate that serves no purpose, is keeping the Church from being relevant in the 21st century. Such groups are holding back the Church. They have put forth an online publication, "The Answers Research Journal," to serve as a forum for research by creationists and scientists that support their position. Their position is consistency with biblical accounts of origins. This is hurting the Church do to its lack of relevancy. How the world was made is irrelevant to the Church. The important question for the Church to address is of an existential nature, Why are we here, and What is our purpose?"

The Language of God by Francis Collins enters into a discussion of the Big Bang Theory. This discussion is foolish and unnecessary because faith has little to do with origins and more to do with potentiality, an unfolding future. Collins also raises the question, "What came before the Big Bang" (Collins, 66)? Who cares? This question is only important for someone trying to rationalize God from a science-based perspective not a faith-based one. He says, "Does such an astonishing event as the Big Bang fit the definition of a miracle" (Collins, 66)? Collins might as well asked, how many angels can dance on the head of a pin?

Ultimately, it does not matter how the universe came to be. All that matters is who are we among the stars? And what is the role of the Church? And what is the place of humanity in the cosmos?

Before going any further, it is imperative at this point to define the Church. To discern the Church's role in society, it is important to know what it is.

According to theologian and martyr Dietrich Bonhoeffer, there are certain ethical imperatives that should drive the Church. First, the demand placed upon those who belong to God's church is not that they should live lives of piety, but that they shall be witnesses to Jesus Christ before the world. For the Church today, that means bearing witness not only to the world in general but to the culture deeply seeded with technology. Second, just because there is darkness and evil in the world, it does not mean the world should be abandoned to the "Devil." The world must be claimed for God who has won it by the incarnation of Jesus Christ, his death, and his resurrection. The third ethical driving force of the church is the summoning of the world into the fellowship of the body of Christ, where truth already belongs. And fourth, God and the world come together in Christ in such a way that despite the differences between the Church and the world a static and "spatial" line of separation between them cannot exist (Bonhoeffer, 201). An amiable conflict must exist.

By focusing solely on biblical faith leading to the hereafter without any application of faith in the world, the Reformers, Bonhoeffer surmises, radically removed God from the world, preparing the way for the growth of the rational and empirical sciences in the 17th and 18th centuries, a time when faith began being replaced by a rationalized and mechanized world.

Now, in light of a "rationalized" and "mechanized" world, Bonhoeffer believed limits must be placed on governments and other institutions which included science. A central responsibility of the Church is to make sure those limits, as set by Christ, remain in place. The Church must be willing to provide the Divine, "No," to science when it exceeds its limitations.

What is the Church to look like in this technological, postmodern? In *The Cost of Discipleship*, Bonhoeffer uses very simple, biblical images to describe the function of the Church—salt, lamps, and baskets. The Church is to follow Matthew 5: 13-16 by serving the world and by being an example to the world, "You are the salt of the earth; but if salt has lost its taste, how can its saltiness be restored? It is no longer good for anything, but is thrown out and trampled under foot. You are the light of the world. A city built on a hill cannot be hid. No one after lighting a lamp puts it under the bushel basket, but on the lamp stand, and it gives light to all in the house. In the same way, let your light shine before others, so that they may see your good works and give glory to your Father in heaven." The disciples are of the earth, salt of the earth not heavenly. They represent the highest good or ideal for this world when lived faithfully. The Church now must live faithfully in order to attract people seeking meaning and a greater purpose. The Church, then, must lead the institutions of the world toward the expression of good for the world, and the Church reminds science when it oversteps its bounds; thus, science in all its applications must be an expression of good. The churches that seem to be growing the most are the ones that are solely personal salvation driven and focused solely on heaven. In the short term, churches grow. In the long term, when face to face with an ever-growing technological world, heaven-bound or pie-in-the-sky churches will collapse by falling into a void of irrelevancy. There is an earthly task that must be carried out. The Church is made of salt, the earth by its very call into serving the world. "The call of Jesus Christ means that we are salt of the earth, or else we are annihilated; either we follow the call or we are crushed beneath it. There is no question of second chance" (Bonhoeffer, 116-17). Bonhoeffer's remarks are prophetic in so much as if the church continues arguing over Creationism/Intelligent Design verses Evolution it will lose its saltiness. If the Church fails to become relevant—or fails to be the "salt of the earth" for the 21st Century—then it will disappear at least in its current form under the weight of mediocrity and irrelevancy. Deep theological reflection is called for now more than ever. Theology should avoid debates, like finding scientific support for Moses' parting of the sea, but instead, reflect upon the liberation of the Hebrews and what that means for humanity, and the painful and joyful realities of every day living with the mind of Christ and thereby raising human consciousness to the knowledge of Divine guidance.

Postmodern theology surrendered nature or the physical world to science; now, it no longer addresses this sense of cosmic loneliness described in Paul. John Haught in an article, "Ecology: Restoring Our Sense of Belonging," talks about the Big Bang in a theological context. It is unimportant for the Church to dwell on whether the Big Bang was the means of creation. Haught says if the universe has a beginning, then, it must have a finite past. It is clear, then, to understand the universe as an unfolding story. The universe and humanity may be seen as "homeless wanderers" (Haught, 2).

Pope John Paul II in his address to the Pontifical Academy of sciences called, *Faith can Never Conflict with Reason*, raised this question "How are we to reconcile the explanation of the world?" For John Paul, the first step is recognizing that "the whole is more than the sum of its parts" (Pope John Paul, 1992, 1-2). In other words, the scientific understanding of life, like how the brain operates, does not exclude the soul; science does not prove or disprove church doctrine. With this understanding of the whole being more than the sum of its parts, each discipline—scientific, theological, literary, philosophical and so forth—needs to have a greater awareness of its own nature and purpose. All people must collectively focus on the stature of humanity as well as the natural world from theological and secular perspectives. As contemporary culture is drawn toward science, the need for the Church to define itself over against other disciplines is even greater. The foremost task facing the Church today is to define itself as relevant in an ever increasing technological culture where one has all the information at the push of button.

In his address on faith and reason, Pope John Paul stated that it was a myth that the Church's rejection of Galileo was a rejection of science; rather, it was an error made by theologians who allowed the literal sense of Sacred Scripture to be imposed upon the physical world. The Church tried to eliminate it instead of engaging it and debating it. The Bible does not concern itself with the details of the physical world. Pope John Paul accommodates science and religion by understanding the two as different branches of knowledge which call for different methods of understanding. These two realms of knowledge are not to be understood as opposition, but methodologies unique to each discipline bring out different aspects of reality [that would challenge one another by means of an amiable conflict]. "Our purpose is precisely to discern and to make known, in the present state of science and within its proper limits, what can be regarded as an acquired truth or at least as enjoying such a degree of probability that it would be imprudent and unreasonable to reject it. In this way, unnecessary conflict can be avoided" (Pope John Paul, 1992, 4-5). This is precisely where the Church risks losing relevancy. Pope John Paul acknowledges that culture is becoming more scientific, but then, if the institutional Church begins accommodating science by avoiding all conflict, it will find itself accommodating itself out of existence. To his credit, he acknowledged the potential dangers associated with science and science, also, must accommodate theology. The Church must be involved in other scientific disciplines, such as biogenetics. Recent discoveries and their possible applications directly affect humanity more so than ever before in thought and action " ...to the point of seeming to threaten the very basis of what is human" (Pope John Paul, 1992, 5). In January of 2008, the United Methodist Church announced its opposition to scientists using skin cells of two men to create cloned embryos. It is unknown if the embryos would have been viable if planted in a womb. The announcement came from Stemagen, a bio-tech company in San Diego, on January 18, 2008. The cloning, according to the company, is intended to create cells that could be used by patients suffering from various diseases. The official position of the church is twofold: first, it calls for a ban on creating waste embryos for the sole purpose of experimentation and disposal; and second, it calls for a ban on all forms of human cloning, according to the United Methodist Church 2008 Book of Discipline. The denomination does not rule out genetic research, and it welcomes, as stated in the denomination's *Social Principles,* the use of genetic technology for improving the health, environmental, and food needs of humanity. This is a good example of one role the Church has in our technological society. United Methodist Church's statement clearly sets boundaries or limits on science; however, while it is calling for a ban on cloning, the denomination additionally states that "Appropriate social and governmental bodies must monitor and guide research and developments in the field. Concern for profit and commercial advantage should be balanced by consideration for individual rights, the interest of wide constituencies, and the common good of future generations" (Arkansas United Methodist, 1). Here, the Church has surrendered its role to the secular world. It turned over its ethical mandate to make sure "individual rights" are met as well as "the common good of future generations." If this responsibility is turned over to "social and governmental bodies," what then is the place of the Church? Does it serve in an appointment capacity where it identifies a problem and turns it over to a secular agency? Here is where relevancy is threatened by not taking a direct, hands-on role in scientific, technological affairs as well as political and economic ones. When it comes to the Church accommodating science, Pope John Paul does believe it is a two-way street. Humanity has two modes of development. One is a horizontal aspect of humanity and creation. This is basically worldly which includes culture, scientific research, technology, and so on. The second is a vertical dimension which transcends the world and humanity. People turn to the One who is the Creator of all. This brings meaning to existence and action for living. The scientist who takes the two to heart, according to Pope John Paul, finds harmony. "Einstein used to say, 'what is eternally incomprehensible in the world is that it is comprehensible.' This intelligibility, attested to by the marvelous discoveries of science and technology leads us to that transcendent and primordial thought imprinted on all things" (Pope John Paul, 1992, 5).

Pope John Paul admonishes science to " ...make every effort to respect the primacy of ethics in your work" (Pope John Paul, 1997, 1). Science is to be ever mindful of methods and discoveries, and knowledge must be joined to conscience. In other words, is it moral to use scientific knowledge gained from Nazi Germany's experimentation on Jews? Here is where the amiable conflict between religion and science begins. The Church sets the limits of moral and ethical behavior and conduct, and it makes sure science and technology do not exceed those limits. Science, on the other hand, must push back against the Church by presenting its case in such a way that its research is for the benefit of humanity. This push and pull between science and religion bring about policy that truly benefits all. Religion and science must battle its way to the point where both can acknowledge the connection between beauty and order in the universe and its link to human dignity. This becomes a reflection of God's glory and imprint on Creation. "It is my prayer that the cause of humanity is authentically served only if knowledge is joined to conscience" (John Paul, 1997, 2). An example of knowledge not being joined to conscience can be seen in the Industrial Revolution which represented technological advancement of its time. The working conditions of the poor masses were horrific—make as much money as possible no matter the human. Some of that price was the loss of human life and destruction of families. The rich got richer and the poor got poorer. The Church must be the voice of the poor. Technology can leave the poor behind. Children in homes that can afford computers have a clear advantage over children who do not have computers in the home. Knowledge is power. Without access to the worldwide web, one does not have power. Pope John Paul does seem to seek a reconciliation and cooperation between science and faith in an address, "The Problems of Science are the Problems of Man," before the *L'Osservatore Romano* as far back as on April 3, 1979.

Pope John Paul makes it clear that the world of science falls under God's sovereignty by identifying two problems on this issue before us: 1) what is the nature of science; and 2) what is the nature of science and faith/religion? Again, in an address delivered on March 30, 1979 he shows a push toward reconciliation by including science under the umbrella of faith. Here, Pope John Paul introduces what I call an "amiable conflict." Everything we discover pays tribute to God, he says. Science, operating under the hand of God, discovers and puts to use its discoveries for the betterment of humanity (Pope John Paul, 1979, 2). It is when science exceeds this limit of service to human beings such as the Nazi experiments on the Jews that the Church steps in and delivers a resounding "No," but before science even gets to that point, the Church must be in constant dialogue, even in conflict but an amiable conflict where both parties sit at the table, where the Church reminds science that it falls under God's domain , just as humanity should be reminded of God's sovereignty; furthermore, while science reminds the Church not to take a literal understanding nor try to prove the Bible scientifically, but rather acknowledge that the goals are essentially the same—a better world. "In order to prevent science and technique from becoming slaves to the will for power of tyrannical forces, political as well as economic, and in order positively to ordain science and technique to the advantage of man, what is necessary, as is usually said, is a supplement of soul, a new breath of spirit, faithfulness to the moral norms that regulate man's life" (Pope John Paul, 1979, 2). There can be no doubt that Pope John Paul understands science as being a tool created by God for humanity's use. Like all gifts, it must be used wisely. Science discovers and puts to use its knowledge in service to humanity by causing humanity and nature to grow at the same time, by humanizing more while respecting and perfecting nature, by bringing to light environmental abuses creating ecological imbalances which in turn causes harm to humanity, and by acknowledging to the world that nature is not a slave to be abused and used but rather to inspire (Pope John Paul, 1979, 2). Science and faith can cooperate even though there is conflict. The two can work toward the cause of peace. Knowledge, ethically speaking, is in service to humanity. In a 1985 address to an international group of scientists taking part in the Marcel Grossman Meeting on Relativistic Astrophysics, Pope John Paul praises science for adding to human knowledge and to the possibilities of peace pertaining to that knowledge. Church and science can serve side by side in friendship, mutual support, and to the benefit of humanity, while maintaining a level of conflict that is healthy and not destructive. Scientific discovery affects human beings on much shorter time frame. It seems like something new is discovered or developed on a daily basis which is why the Church should not be too friendly with science because a cautious, vigilant eye must be kept on technological developments. History shows tools can be abused. With one eye on science, the other eye should be focused on humanity and its institutions. One could say that if science is a tool from God, then, why should it be monitored? The answer is twofold: 1) real presence of chaos in the world, and 2) human free will.

Psalm 8 describes how God gave humanity dominion over the earth. Dominion is a tool for regulating or monitoring; in addition, dominion, under the wrong circumstances, can easily become domination without checks and balances. Leaving God out of this human partnership has disastrous results. Signs of ecological disasters are all around us from the subtle eroding of top soil to the increasing destructive forces of hurricanes to the melting of polar ice. Psalm 8 reminds us that God's care and humanity's care for the earth are in one accord. So, just as Pope John Paul saw science as a tool. Conflict can be seen as a tool as well. The conflict between the Jewish community and the Matthean community as seen in the Gospel of Matthew brought about a better understanding of discipleship for the Matthean community and Christianity as a whole. The conflict Paul had with the other disciples eventually led to the early Church embracing the gentiles. The early Church's conflict with Gnosticism led to the development of doctrine, and Martin Luther's conflict with the Holy Roman Catholic Church expanded the church and unfortunately and unknowingly contributed to the Enlightenment, a period of time when humanity began to compartmentalized human endeavor. These early church conflicts were far from friendly; however, today, in an age of instantaneous communication and a worldwide media, the Church's conflict with science must be a friendly one and yet still a conflict.

In an address delivered on October 28, 1994, to the Pontifical Academy of Sciences, Pope John Paul places upon science and puts forward an amiable conflict between religion and science that centers upon the "human person." He wants to place limits on science while acknowledging science as a tool for improving society, " ...the questions that our society is facing increasingly need to be illumined by the sciences, which are one of the prized resources or our constantly evolving and changing world." It is interesting to note that once again the Pope uses "evolution" in his address; most importantly, he continues this statement by placing boundaries upon science, "However, at the same time, one should not lose sight of the fact that science alone cannot claim to account for the transcendent origin and ultimate purpose of human existence" (Pope John Paul, 1994, 1). Science is a tool for benefiting humanity. Genome sequencing will create new paths of research for healing purposes—cures for various illnesses, prevention of genetic diseases, and a further understanding of the physiological aspect of people. Within these boundaries, science is truly a device for improving the human condition. When science exorcises unrestrained freedom, a purely scientific explanation of human freedom without utilitarian purposes and goals, this diminishes and even takes away human freedom thus exceeding or going beyond its limits Science cannot use a person's medical data and information contained in the genome to be exploited by society. For example, an embryo with indications of a severe genetic defect might be terminated by the mother with due cause, but genetic testing may reveal a propensity toward addictive behaviors. However, what if traits the parents do not want appear? Should the embryo be terminated? Others boundaries Pope John Paul puts on science is that science should take into account the metaphysical, ethical, social and legal questions faced by conscience in which the principals of reason clarifies. Knowledge must be put to the service of moral truth. Pope John Paul calls for the establishment of ethics committees for reflection and consideration of the ethical and moral aspects of research (Pope John Paul, 1994, 2). What is the role of the Church? The Church should be independent of any ethical committee established within the scientific community in order to operate without influence.

In contrary to Hannah Arendt as mentioned in chapter 2 who believes science dehumanizes humanity, Pope John Paul in sum believed scientific achievements proclaim the dignity of the human being and brings light to humanity's role in the universe. He tried to seek cooperation between the two with minimal conflict. Finally, when scientists humbly search for the secrets of nature, God will lead them there, according to Pope John Paul's theological understanding of the role of science and religion in a postmodern age. Faith does not add to research, but science meets, in nature, the presence of the Creator. Here, is where the Church must remind them. Pope John Paul was correct to say that scientific achievements proclaim the dignity of people, but he fails to acknowledge the potential dangers associated with scientific advancement. He failed to identify that one of the roles of the Church is to keep an eye on progress in order to make sure science does in fact elevate humanity.

In sum, a devastating consequence of science is its potential for dehumanizing people. For example, through brain imaging, science is able to locate the will and passions, which challenges religious concepts of the soul. "Brain chemists track imbalances that could account for ecstatic states of visionary saints or, some suggest, of Jesus" (Biema, p. 50). The Incarnation meant Jesus became flesh and blood in order to not only assure salvation but to elevate humanity to a higher ground through a sacrificial love ethic as lived and died for by Jesus Christ. Science is now reducing humanity down to genetic mapping and bio-chemicals. Acts of bravery, compassion, and love have biological motivations, according to recent scientific studies. Over the last few decades, a field of study referred to as evolutionary psychology has emerged. Basically, it reduces morality and altruistic acts as behavioral adaptations for the preserving of genes and the forwarding of those genes into the future. The opposite, for the body does not distinguish, is also true for negative genetic characteristics. If this is the case, one will eventually argue that a person who has a genetic propensity toward violence, a genetic defect or a birth defect, may assault or even murder without claiming responsibility. This questions the very notion of one's accountability for committing a crime—"I was born this way." This belief system essentially eliminates concepts of good and evil. Every action has biological roots. Good and evil are neutral concepts. How do we as a society account for Adolph Hitler or serial killers or gunmen on a shooting rampage? The logical conclusion would be to execute every criminal from petty theft to murder in order to eliminate the bad gene pool. If it could be proven that Adolph Hitler had damaged or defective genes, does that de-criminalize his horrific acts of violence?

One apparent concern that needs to be raised in regards to science and technology is the social isolation; for example, in a newspaper article titled, "Fisher of Men Uses Net to Reach Out to Worshippers," appearing in the *Arkansas Democrat-Gazette*, describes an online-only church calling itself the "Little Rock Net Church." The services are conducted from the living room of the Rev. Jim Brettell who discovered that current online churches are simply live-streaming video from their sanctuaries. Not only is Brettell's sermon delivered, the Rev. Brettell holds communion services as well. People sign up by choosing a user name and password. As of February, 2008, the church has forty-two active members and ninety-one honorary members. One of the active members [it is difficult to determine how one is actively involved in an online church.] as quoted by the newspaper liked the service because he did not have to leave the house to go to church. He added it was convenient to watch the service at his leisure. Rev. Brettell said this is one of the best ways to reach people (Hahn, p. 6B). The problem is Brettell's focus on the individual rather than the community. Church is not solely about worship; the formation of real, authentic community is essential to the gathered believers. For example a recent study shows that 12 to 40 percent of people with an osteoporotic hip fracture will die within six months. Depression is a main factor for this statistic because the elderly become depressed and less active (Neustadt, 1). It is the community of faith that can make a difference not medical science. The Church can encourage the elderly to eat right and to be active by bringing meals to the home or giving them rides to church activities. Here, the Church can be just as involved in the healing process as physicians and surgeons.

The newspaper article cited a Barna Group study. It projected back in 2001 that fifty million people would rely on the internet for their religious and spiritual needs by the end of the decade. Furthermore, a hundred million people will seek religious teachings online. "'Fifty million Americans seem to be a pretty big barrel to fish in for the rest of my life. These people are not leaving the church. They are leaving traditional church,'" said Rev. Brettell (Hahn, 6B). This last part of Brettell's quotation is very telling. Here, we see Arendt's fears actualized. Technology has replaced real, human interaction. How can Christians understand the incarnation and the spiritual struggles of life in community from behind a computer screen?

It is apparent that the technology which drives culture is now driving religious life. Since the Enlightenment, challenges from science have arisen that have a direct impact upon the Church. First, scientific method called into question any truth claim made outside of the physical, observable world. The Church has bought into this; for example, the co-opting of scientific language into the vocabulary of the Church. Second, science demolished biblical cosmology that existed for fifteen hundred years. Charles Darwin dropped a bomb in 1859 which challenged the Church's notion that humans descended from Adam and Eve. This was not such a bad thing because it shifted attention away from a biblical literalism of creation, and opened the door—whether the Church chooses to walk through it or not—for the Church to redefine itself in a relevant way by arguing biblical cosmology does not advance humanity. In fact, it is divisive. Liberals accept evolution, and fundamentalists reject it. The Church is divided for the wrong reasons However, arguing the place of humanity within a technologically-driven world is productive and promotes the needs of humanity. And third, much of the West questions anything supernatural because of postmodern psychiatry. Miracles are questioned even by believers. And four, nature has become a self-contained, determined causal system. There is no freedom, no meaning, and no value. The universe needed no God to create it. The Big Bang explains it all, and the mystery is removed. Creation is really an accidental coming together of atoms (Cauthen, 2). Thus, humanity is the result of one giant accident, one cosmic clash of atoms. Science does not give meaning to life. The Church can and must provide that meaning in a communal context because only in community can we be shaped and formed.

Currently, there are two main responses to science: fundamentalism and liberalism. Fundamentalism sees the bible as inerrant, having no error. There can be no compromise on biblical truths. Any contradictive arguments against the bible are seen as blasphemous. The other response is liberalism. Liberal theology embraces science by believing the realm of science belongs solely to science, and do not challenge science on its own terms. The Church simply must come to an understanding with science, and basically, most liberal theologians acknowledge two spheres of realities, theological and scientific. Two different worlds are dealt with in two different ways. One gives value, meaning, purpose, and freedom. The other makes truth claims about the observable world (Cauthen, 4).

The best way to consider science and religion is not to make sharp distinctions between facts and values because the two relate to each and must be kept in tension, in an amiable conflict. Instead of a dualistic world, this approach speaks of different dimensions to the same event. Science gives us a partial picture, one perspective of the whole. It cannot provide a complete description of reality. Science is only one dimension of a reality that can be measured. Theology can provide the moral and religious dimensions of the whole. From out of the conflict between the two, completeness and wholeness can be achieved.

There are two aspects to religion that science cannot address nor provide an answer: community and its role in people's lives and a language for personal trials and tribulations.

Social sciences may be able to provide and explanation, but it cannot create community. Neither can science create authentic, caring community. The Church is the one social entity that has the capacity to do, so albeit its track record has been one of trial and error, and it has shown its rejection of community through exclusionary measure, but that is not the real church. The Israelites used dietary laws and circumcision to exclude others. The early Church was open to all, but unfortunately, as the Church grew, so did its desire to keep others out. With all that said, the Church has the mechanisms for authentic community where people can find meaning and purpose and shared experiences. Email and text messaging and chat rooms do not allow the individual to fully express him and her. Chat rooms may reflect diversity in blogging and messaging, but it lacks the face-to-face encounter that overcomes things like prejudices and bigotries. Community embraces diversity. When a Church community welcomes all regardless of gender, race, nationality, ethnicity, sexual orientation and trans-gendered, then, the bonds that hold society together are strengthened. Paul writes in Galatians 3:28, "There is no longer Jew or Greek; there is no longer slave or free; there is no longer male or female; for all you are one in Christ Jesus." Pastor and twentieth-century theologian Dietrich Bonhoeffer writes in his book, *Life Together,* about the necessity of Christian fellowship. He makes several important points about living in community. He sees community as, "The Christian, however, must bear the burden of a brother. He must suffer and endure the brother. It is only when he is a burden that another person is really a brother and not merely an object manipulated" (Bonhoeffer, 100). This is the essence of community. Here, science cannot tread.

Science, with all its accumulated knowledge, lacks the language of grief and human trials and tribulations. For example, one receives news that he or she has inoperable, pancreatic cancer. Science can explain it and even attempt to treat it, but it cannot inspire a person to overcome it. The Church makes the claim that a person can do all things through Christ who strengthens him or her. When one believes God is with them, when one believes the community backs them, tremendous healing whether physical, emotional or spiritual takes place. The Church can provide a language to assist people during their trials, and even a language to help those to die. Again, science cannot tread here.

In sum, science-technology cannot provide an answer to why we must struggle. Randy Pausch is a college professor who was diagnosed with pancreatic cancer and was given only a few months to live. He was married and the father of two small children. In early 2008, he delivered a speech on the *Oprah Winfrey Show* the same farewell lecture he gave to his students.

The lecture was not about death, but rather about life. He talked about how struggles can lead to victories depending on your attitude. Science cannot create an attitude. He asked the crowd, "Are you a Tigger or an Eeyore" from Winnie the Pooh? In other words, are you a complainer whenever life's obstacles hit you, or are you bouncing around running into obstacles and yet bouncing forward maintaining your happiness? Science does not ask nor cannot it answer such questions, but religion can.

One of the things Professor Pausch said that was helpful was his understanding that the brick walls of life are not intended to stop us, but to help us reach our dreams. In other words, obstacles can be essential for growth. Thus, church and science must collide in order to reach the dream of a better world.

Let's put this in a theological perspective. We are often faced with brick walls in life. You can't climb over; you can't go around or underneath. You have to break through it. It usually hurts to crash through a wall, but on the other side of it, you are stronger bodily, mentally, and spiritually. Science does not inspire, but belief in God provides the necessary strength to conquer. Science cannot appeal to internal fortitude.

Here is story that is commonly told about struggle. A little boy found a caterpillar while playing in the garden. He picked it up and took it inside to show his mother. The boy kept it as a pet in a large jar. He gave it some leaves and little sticks to climb.

One day, the caterpillar climbed up one of the sticks and hung upside down. The mother explained that the caterpillar was creating a cocoon and would soon turn into a butterfly.

One day he notices a small hole in the cocoon, and the butterfly started to come out, but it struggled to come out through the hole, and so the little boy helped it by making the hole wider. The butterfly quickly emerged. However, it was very swollen with shriveled wings. The wings never expanded to fly, so it died. Without the struggle, the fluid was stuck in its body, and the wings were never fully developed for flight.

Struggle is a part of life. Science wants to take away life's struggles by making life as easy and convenient as possible through technological advancements, but the struggle helps define who we are. The Apostle Paul knew that in his letter to the Hebrews, " ...after you had been enlightened, you endured a hard struggle with sufferings, sometimes publicly exposed to abuse and persecution ..." Paul goes on to describe the importance of struggling, "For you need endurance, so that when you have done the will of god, you may receive what is promised" (Hebrews 10:32, 36). Paul is saying you will hit brick walls, and it will hurt, but if you keep struggling you can break through the wall. Science wants to remove brick walls. Make life easier. Take away struggles. This is the failure of science. Easier does not necessarily meant better when there are no more obstacles to overcome. Brick walls define who we are and who we are not.

The Letter of James shines a lot of light on the issue of struggle, "my brothers and sisters, whenever you face trials of any kind, consider it nothing but joy, because you know that the testing of your faith produces endurance; and let endurance have its full effect, so that you may be mature and complete, lacking in nothing" (James 1:2-4).

Notice James says, "When you face trials," not if you face trials.

In other words, we can expect trials and hard times. God did not promise that His people are removed from the struggles of life. In fact, from a biblical perspective, struggles help forge us or make who we are as human. James also says that trials and struggles are a part of life intended not to destroy us but to develop us and strengthen us. Remember, professor paunch who said bricks walls are not to stop us, but to help us fulfill our dreams.

In our struggles, we develop perseverance. Life's struggles are grueling, but because of them, we find ourselves becoming stronger and more confident. We discover who we are, and grow as human beings.

Also, notice the last part of James, " ...so that you may be mature and complete." through life's struggles we are made complete, or have a healthy balance because our bodies, minds, and spirits are what we bring to life's struggles—similar to working muscles. When you work beyond the comfort zone, your muscles grow. We grow too when enduring trials and tribulations. Even when life crushes us, because of grace, we can emerge, like the butterfly, beautiful and strong. We can emerge a well-balanced person of mind, body, and spirit. Science cannot address all three of these human aspects, especially by denying the spirit. It is the spirit that sees us through the struggles of life. Science and technology want to make life easier, but at what cost?

Struggles are an essential part to being a human being. It was not science and technology that made the World War II generation the greatest generation. It was how they endured struggles and overcame them. The Church can teach children about life, and all its struggles as well as overcoming trials one may face by faith. Children can overcome hardships and struggles through the power of community as manifested in the Church and God. The struggle makes us who we are. The Church teaches us and forms character whereas science and technology cannot. For this very reason, both need to be a part of the human experience and in conflict with one another.

Where, then, is the tension between science and religion? Astrophysicist Robert Jastrow believes there should be no tension. The problem lies with a misunderstanding of both. Tension should not exist because each discipline deals with different realms of human thought, such as, religion deals with the uniqueness and diverseness of humanity, and science sees people as one organism among many. John Haught, professor of theology at Georgetown University, agrees with Jastrow in the sense that there is no inherent conflict between the two, but the two kinds of belief systems are the nature of the conflict (Think Tank, 2). Physicists and theologians try to reconcile this conflict by saying that the two address different areas of thought. People of faith believe in the sovereignty of God which includes science under God's dominion, and people, as partners in creation, must oversee science as part of God's created order. By definition of purpose, science and church cannot be separated. There is an underlying assumption here that conflict is bad, and it must be eliminated, and today that elimination is brought on about by science co-opting religion, and the religion's surrendering of the natural world to science.

The nature of this conflict is not Evolution vs. Creation, but rather it is the diminishment of humanity verses its place above all creation according to the Psalmist. Such issues as homosexuality and abortions are not the real enemy facing the Church. The real concerns come from science and technology that seems to provide more and more answers to the questions of life, diminishing the role of the Church. A word of caution here, it is important not to reduce Jesus as a moral example—a wise teacher, a friend, and so forth—who provides all the answers to life. Francis S. Collins in his book, *The Language of God,* points out that the concept of right and wrong appears to be universal with perhaps different outcomes. He raises the question on whether or not right and wrong is an "intrinsic" quality of humans or the result of cultural traditions. Collins misses the point of faith. Anyone can follow moral laws of some sort, and anyone can demonstrate altruism. What distinguishes faith or belief from the secular is how moral law is employed and to what ends. The apostle Paul in the seventh chapter of Romans reveals his inner conflict between adhering to the law and the law of grace. The law provides a moral compass and is a creation of God; however, it is that same moral law found in the Old Testament and quoted in the New Testament that Paul used to justify his persecution of those early. Sin or chaos corrupted his ability to live out the law, but it is the love and grace of Christ that overcomes sin and brings order to chaos, "For I know that nothing good dwells in me, [Here, Paul is clear that he is corrupted by sin.] that, is in my flesh. I can will what is right [i.e. follow moral law], but I cannot do it. For I do not do the good I want, but the evil I do not want is what I do" (Romans 7:18-19). Even though God has given moral laws, Paul believed, it takes a conversion of the heart to properly follow the law. One can follow the law, according to Paul, but without love, the law or any other moral behavior is in vain, " …therefore, love is the fulfilling of the law" (Romans 13:10); "Let all that you do be done in love" (1 Corinthians 16:14); and Paul says the greatest of all spiritual gifts is love. Without love, moral law can be meaningless. Religion teaches the way to love exceedingly, and any biological definition falls short of the meaning and purpose of love.

Therefore, the Church must be the body of Christ in a real, radical, earth-shaking way. The Church must be the embodiment of Christ and that embodiment is love and grace. These things supersede any moral law that may be intrinsic to being human. Science, for the most part, does not set out with intent to diminish humanity's place in the universe. Its intentions are noble, but science and technology are not single-mindedly concerned with the stature of men and women. It is the Church's role to make sure science is aware the effect it is having on humanity and the observable world. Somebody has to say "No." Likewise, the Church must constantly be aware of its own motivations. Pope John Paul said science is by itself unable to take into account the transcendent origin and ultimate purpose of human existence. This is where the Church steps into the amiable conflict. The certitude of science must be seen in relation to the whole truth about men and women (Pope John Paul, 1994, 1). Maintaining such tension or conflict is essential to human freedom and uniqueness more so now than ever before. Scientific knowledge and technological application has become the driving force of culture; however, it does not always improve the living conditions of people. Technology often widens the gap between rich and poor, and it gave rise to the military industrial complex as defined by President Dwight Eisenhower. Science and technology can be misused to manipulate humanity for economic and political control. Often forgotten, science is connected to the Nazi horrific and torturous treatment of the Jews. The same can be said about religion, especially among militant Islamists who seek to derail economic and political systems; they became agents of chaos, and even, agents of evil, such as those who shoot *Planned Parenthood* physicians. By having an amiable conflict, both church or religion and science are reminded of their respective potentials for abuses. Through this amiable conflict both science and religion are better for it. For people of faith, it is tempting to reduce one's "personal relationship with Jesus" as the core of Christianity. Christians want to get comfortable with God like a well worn recliner chair. This diminishes God because the God of the cosmos and cannot be self contained.

This faith vs. science debate is important enough to make the cover of the November 13, 2006 *Time* magazine, and the decline and fall of Christianity was featured in the April 13, 2009 addition of *Newsweek*. The *Time* cover story featured a debate between atheist biologist Richard Dawkins and Christian geneticist Francis Collins. Unfortunately, the debate focused upon Evolution vs. Creationism and the entire Intelligent Design concept. Again, this is a misdirected debate. The Church should simply surrender the mechanics of how humanity came to be to science while embracing the existential component of Genesis 1 and 2. Genesis raises more questions than what it answers, so it is those very questions that strike at the heart of humanity, and humanity's place and purpose in the universe. Americans wrestle with that very question, and also Americans embrace science while attending church or synagogue or mosque. People want both medical technology and miracles. When medicine fails, they hope for a Hail Mary (Beima, p. 50).

Science and faith must be in conflict with each other because of their natures. Science will never answer the existential questions of Genesis. Religion will never provide concrete, full-proof explanations of how the universe was made, for that is not the purpose of faith. Science seeks to harmonize and unify, and especially, to make comfortable. The Church is the opposite because it intrudes in people's lives. It thrusts itself into people's lives without reason, permission, and yes, unwelcome. Jesus speaks of his intrusion, "Do not think that I have come to bring peace to the earth; I have not come to bring peace, but a sword. For I have come to set a man against his father, and a daughter against her mother, and a daughter-in-law against her mother-in-law; and one's foes will be members of one's own household" (Matthew 11:34-39). Jesus' intention here is to redefine family. No longer does biology or genetics define family. Family is anyone who does the will of God, and the will of God is firmly rooted in love. The Church does not come to unify culture, which includes science and technology, but rather to challenge it. Science needs to be challenged in order to make it better for humanity and to prevent it from reducing people to genetic material under a microscope.

Ultimately, it is foolish for the Church to convince the scientific community of the existence of God. Some scientists may believe and others won't. Likewise, science would waste its time trying to disprove the existence of God. Both must remain in conflict servings checks and balances for the betterment of humanity. Yale psychologist Paul Bloom has written "'Religion and science will always clash.'" God's existence is either true or not, but if God exists out of space and time and on occasion steps out of eternity and into human time, scientific tools cannot be employed on something that is outside the known world (Beima, 50).

Francis Collins, geneticist, believes there is nothing inherently in conflict between the idea of a creator God and what science has revealed about creation. There is an existential difference. God chose to act in the world, but we will never know why or how. It is like asking God what God was doing before creating the universe—there are some things that humanity does not need to know.

God is the god of the paradox. Collins uses logic to prove an illogical God. God exists beyond all human reason; thus, any human created, or earthbound description of God and God's actions in the world fall short. The Apostle Paul's words are important to remember, when he describes the power of God and how God destroys " ...the wisdom of the wise, and the discernment of the discerning I will thwart. Where is the one who is wise? Where is the scribe? Where is the debater of this age? Has not God made foolish the wisdom of the world?" (1 Corinthians 1:18-20). Paul does not say knowledge and wisdom are useless and should be discarded. By using the word, "foolish," he is making a powerful statement. Today, we see a fool as someone who is stupid or idiotic. In the Bible, foolishness has a very serious history. Someone who ridicules God or disregards God's laws is foolish. Jesus said in Matthew 5:22, "If you say, 'You fool,' you will be liable to the hell of fire." At the very minimum science should take Paul's passage in 1 Corinthians to heart by using it as a moral and ethical measuring stick. God's laws are about people and relationships with one another in community and with the Divine. The wisdom of the world is foolish because the world's wisdom involves wants and gets at all costs.

The world is driven by greed, lust, and envy which fall under the general heading of power. Science one day may find the genes to explain such motivations and behavior, but science cannot stop it. The Church specifically and religion generally can keep the human desire for power and control in check. The Qohlet, or Teacher, writes in the seventh chapter of Ecclesiastes that a wise person approaches life and all its experiences with a strong sense of mortality. He or she should be more aware that death is the finality for all people. All behavior must be guided by the reality or our own mortality. This forces one to pursue knowledge from the human perspective because death is the one of two shared experiences by all people. The best perspective a person can hope to achieve in life is the perspective of its possible outcome, as demonstrated by King Ahab's message to the King of Aram in the Old Testament, "One who puts on armor should not brag like one who takes it off (1 Kings 20:11).

Chapter 4: Beyond Hard Sciences

Without our egos the universe would be absolutely clean, all the animals and rocks and spiders and moon-rocks and stars and grains of sand absolutely doing their thing, unself-consciously (Rabbit Redux, 143).

Perhaps a saving grace for the Church will ironically come from science in the form of the theoretical sciences. The farther scientists move from the core/hard sciences—biology, chemistry, physics and so forth—the closer they come to the spiritual or even the Divine. For instance, just as the Church imports words like "evolution" and "DNA" into its vocabulary, the theoretical sciences will often use God language in its vocabulary, such as the "God Particle." The "God Particle" is believed to be a mysterious, sub-atomic fragment or splinter that permeates the entire universe, and the particle has the potential to explain how everything is the way it is. It has been described as God's hidden signature on Creation. Nobody has seen this particle, and physicists are trying to develop an experiment to reveal it by causing a cataclysmic explosion of heat, light, and radiation in order to recreate the conditions right before the Big Bang. The explosion hopefully will reveal many things one of which is the "God Particle." The "God Particle" is called the *Higgs boson* particle named after Peter Higgs who first proposed the concept in the 1960s. It is unclear how this particle works or how it interacts with all other forms of matter to give them their mass. This could help explain how energy and mass are related. Margaret Wertheim sat on a discussion panel hosted by PBS that addressed the conflict between science and religion. She said God is appearing more and more in the work of theoretical scientists, and they are becoming the theologians of the modern age (Think Tank, 3). Here lies the danger; theology, once solely the realm of religion, can easily become part of the realm of science, and soon thereafter, religion is gone at least in the way we know it.

On the other hand, religion/theology can play an important role in this postmodern age of rapid scientific and technological advancements. Science and religion should remain separate, at odds even, but equally important for describing reality from various angles of human existence. Science and religion need to be pushed beyond their own limitations, beyond their own experiences and into a realm that is totally other. One particular area of study where this might occur is with Chaos Theory. There are other theories that might be useful; however, Chaos Theory was made popular by movies, such as *Jurassic Park* where one of the characters played by actor Jeff Goldblum uses Chaos Theory to explain why dinosaurs and people should not live together.

The purpose of science is rather straightforward: it is a branch of study which employs a body of facts or truths that are ordered in such a way that shows the operation of general laws. Science employs facts or principals in order to advance knowledge.

Let us look at Chaos Theory, and how it might be useful to theologians. This theoretical science may be the point at which science and religion overlap. There is no better theological starting point than the question of free will and determinism [or predestination].

For the Church, the concept of free will argues that God allows evil in the world to basically give humanity a choice between good and evil. God allows people to commit evil deeds because God basically wants children not slaves but children often choose to stray. Without freedom in the world, then some people are destined or condemned to do evil acts. There is no choice. Everything is predestined. Predestination simply states that some people are predestined or predetermined to be saved or damned without regard for their merit. Of course, there are many varying definitions and degrees.

One of Chaos Theory's contributions to science is how it challenges the way scientists think about determinism, predictability, and other natural occurring phenomenon from weather to the beating of the human heart to the growth and decline of animal populations. Systems that were once governed by Newtonian laws [which state that a cause can be determined by its effects are always predictable] are now unpredictable. For example, Newton's three laws of motion: the first law states a body stays at rest or remains in motion with a constant speed unless some external force acts upon it; the second law states that the sum of the forces acting on an object equals the product of the mass of the object and the acceleration produced by the forces, with motion in the direction of the ensuing forces; and the third law of motion states that for every action on a body there is an equal and opposite reaction. This is the Newtonian understanding of a predictable or determined world—direct cause and effect. St. Thomas Aquinas believed that the initial motion of history or movement of the stars was caused by an "unmoved mover," who is God. God was the original cause, but in a world such as ours this concept or understanding of God is difficult to translate into our age of science and technology. Science has determined the Big Bang was the initial "push" that got things started. Seeing God solely as the "unmoved mover" risks reducing God to the cosmic watchmaker.

As chaos theory becomes more popularized and as it becomes more understood and applied in even more practical matters, does chaos theory, then, provide for us a new perspective or paradigm on the question of free will and determinism? Chaos Theory and faith intersect at the point of Creation itself. It provides a new way to understand the beauty, fullness, and complexity of God's creative work in the universe and the ordering of the physical realms of existence, i.e. the universe. A temptation exists to claim that the Big Bang is one way to describe how God created the universe, but this is a cosmic, stop watch approach to how God acts in and through the world. The Big Bang suggests that

God acted one time, and then, walked away from his Creation in order to let it evolve on its own. Such understanding removes any attribute of creativity.

Let us now take a brief look at Chaos Theory itself.

Meteorologist at M.I.T., Edward Lorenz, published an article called, "Deterministic Non-periodic Flow," addressing the predictions of long-range weather forecasts by predicting the movement of weather patterns in the atmosphere. These long-term patterns are nearly impossible to accurately predict no matter how many times one tries. Systems, like global weather patterns such as the El Nino effect, are simply too complex to fully predict and understand. There are simply too many variables to accurately predict the future of weather.

Out of Lorenz's publication came the ""Butterfly Effect,"" popularized by Hollywood in recent years. Basically, the flapping of a butterfly's wings in Peking can have a random cascading effect that eventually forms a tornado in Oklahoma. This can be compared to balancing the point of a pencil on a desk top. The slightest touch, a breath, a vibration in any direction would produce a far greater effect on the pencil's ability to remain in balance—the pencil would fall. In other words, a very small change in initial conditions can affect the overall physical system.

The "Butterfly Effect" is sensitive to the dependence on initial conditions. It may be applied to a great variety of systems in the physical world-the human heart beat, the spread of disease through an animal population, the dripping of water droplets from a faucet, the formation of snowflakes, or the behavior of the stock market. Thus, any change at the beginning of any system can be multiplied to produce erratic and unpredictable behavior over time. A swinging pendulum was believed to be the epitome of the Newtonian paradigm of predictability, but it is now known to exhibit "chaotic" and irregular motion patterns under particular conditions, thus, falling outside of Newtonian, linear thought. For mathematical physicist David Pierre Ruelle, chaotic systems are the "paradoxical combination of determinism and long-term unpredictability." Ruelle is a Belgian-French mathematical physicist. He has been involved with statistical physics and dynamical systems, and along with Floris Takens, he coined the terms "strange attractor," and founded a new theory of turbulence. Others added that even simple things can exhibit this tendency (Davis, 1-3). A children's tire swing hung from a tree limb is a perfect example. If certain boundaries are known, one can predict how and where the swing will go. One can predict where the tire swing will be at every point. If one places a boundary condition on a limited or confined system, no accurate predictions can be made. Long range weather forecasts are very uncertain. Certain systems do not obey the laws of physics.

In sum, the ""Butterfly Effect"" is then the tendency of a system to be sensitive to initial conditions. When an unknown variable is introduced at the beginning of a system, it can disrupt the flow of the system, making predictability difficult. A marble placed on a smooth surface can be predicted where it might stop when some force acts upon it to move it. If you place several pebbles on the surface, it becomes more difficult to predict where it might come to a rest. It may hit a pebble or it might not. Systems over periods of time become unpredictable because the longer the system, the increased chances of an outside force or additional variables act upon it; this gives rise to a belief that a butterfly flapping its wings in one area of the world causes a hurricane in the Gulf of Mexico or some other weather event in another remote area of the world. This is not to be compared to the domino effect or a ripple effect in a pond. Dominos operate in a linear fashion where one event directly causes another event. The "Butterfly Effect" amplifies the condition upon each frequentative. Falling dominos is a simple, linear model or system for which A leads to B and to C and so on. In complex, non-linear phenomenon, A does not necessarily lead to B, but it usually does. That is where the unpredictability enters into the equation. One never knows when A will not lead to B.

What then are the implications of Chaos Theory for theology and religion, especially concerning free will and predestination or determinism?

Chaos Theory can be a tool for the exercising of human free will because all humanity operates within complex, fluid systems and sub-systems—international politics and trade, organizations, non-profits, family dynamics, circle of friends, and individual lives from heart beats to interactions with co-workers. Chaos effects humanity at all levels from the lives of individuals to the world wide economy. Theologians of the 21st century must pay close attention to the issue of chance and unpredictability in the world in regards to "God's providential government of the world" (Davis, 4). Albert Einstein knew this was an important point for discussion when he asked, "Does God throw dice?" William Pollard, priest and physicist, answers Einstein with the affirmative: " …only in a world in which the laws of nature govern events in accordance with the casting of dice [i.e. probability] can the biblical view of a world whose history is responsive to God's will prevail." Pollard believes biblical and scientific descriptions were the same events; they are also complimentary, and God allowed chance in the world as part of the divine providence (Davis, 4).

David Bartholomew—author of *God, Chance and Purpose: Can God Have It Both Way?*—believes "chance" is part of God plan for creation. It is a real part of the created order of things, and not to be understood as adversarial. For him, chance can be viewed as God working in the world. "By chance I have found that my *iPod* seems to have moods. When I put it on shuffle mode, sometimes it plays mostly jazz, sometimes mostly classical songs, sometimes mostly pre-classical Gregorian chants and Renaissance music. However, it does seem to me that sometimes my iPod knows which music I want to hear" (Ussery, 11).

The rolling of dice is really about chance. D. J. Bartholemew, author of *God of Chance*, puts forward that chance is a part of creation; it is part of God's Plan: the "grist for the providential mill" and not an obstacle to God's work (Davis, 4-5). Bartholomew also believes that chance is God's tool to get things started similar to Aquinas' unmoved mover. John Davis, professor of systematic theology and Christian ethics at Gordon-Conwell Theology Seminary, believes this has implications for the Creationist-Evolution debate. "The point being made here is that placing chance and chaos within the larger law structures created by God gives an entirely different perspective for understanding the issues of the creation-evolution debate. The 'random variations' of evolutionary biology are then seen as the providential means ordained of God in the process of creation." (Davis, 3-4). Creation never stops, and God continues to create constantly shaping and reshaping, guiding and directing the world until God deems it complete and perfect. Creation stood as a system. Humanity was added to that system making it more complex, and then, the serpent, an ancient symbol for chaos, enters introducing chaos into this perfect, complex system. Adam and Eve exercised their free will, and thus, we have chaos or sin let loose in the world. Now, because of chaos, a curse came upon Creation. The curse in 21st century language was chaos set free in what was once a simple, linear system. Now, Creation is vulnerable to chaos, and its future is unknown by humanity.

Genesis 3:17-18 states that God tells Adam, "Because … you ate from the tree which I had forbidden you to eat, cursed be the soil because of you! … It will yield you thorns and thistles, as you eat the produce of the land." Here, we see the introduction of chaos into agriculture. Farmers cannot predict when the growing season will have ample rain or not, or if it will be a cool or hot summer, or how many thorns and thistles will sprout in the soy bean field, or how many bad seeds are mixed with the good ones.

Paul probably had Genesis 3 in mind when he wrote Romans 8:19 through 25. It was a common belief among Paul's Jewish peers that when Adam disobeyed God's command, and humanity subsequently fell into captivity to sin as well as the entire universe. Not only did men and women "fall" to sin/chaos but all of Creation suffered, and still stands in the need of redemption by the elimination of chaos. And what is redemption? For nature, it is a return to that state of perfection similar to the time prior to Adam's guilt, a time when chaos was not present.

Nature is restlessly waiting for fulfillment and meaning and completion. Creation longs to once again be restored to that perfect system where nature and humanity are unified as one Creation. Paul writes, "We know that the whole creation has been groaning in labor pains until now; and not only the creation, but we ourselves groan …" (Romans 8:22). Nature is isolated from that perfect relationship with God and humans, and it finds itself in an unpredictable universe. Out of nature's loneliness it groans and moans; the wind wails; the seas sigh.

Paul tells us we already have the first fruits or the first installment of the Spirit that came at Pentecost. It brought with it the ordering of chaos, and now we are waiting for the redemption of our bodies, or in other words, that last installment of the Spirit which makes us complete and whole and no longer a victim of chaos. Pentecost was another act of Creation pushing the universe toward perfection and completion and the elimination of chaos, "And suddenly from heaven there came sound like the rush of a violent wind, and it filled the entire house where they were sitting. Divided tongues, as of fire, appeared among them, and a tongue rested on each of them. ... And as this sound the crowd gathered and was bewildered, because each one heard them speaking in the native language of each" (Acts 2:1-8). In other words, we see God bringing order to chaos. God's final victory is the destruction or elimination of chaos from the universe.

Paul informs the early Christian movement that since we have hope through the first fruits or first installment of the Spirit at Pentecost, we come to expect that something far greater than anything we have ever known is waiting for us. And like nature, we too groan inwardly and wait for that restoration. The Second Letter of Peter also says to wait patiently for this restored relationship—a new heaven and a new earth freed from chaos by the destruction of the primordial seas as described in the Book of Revelation—for it is there where righteousness shall dwell, a perfect state without chaos. The human system, including the natural world, is purged of chaos.

How chance might pertain to humanity's freewill, and how God uses chance might be as follow. A chance car accident leads to the conversion of a reckless individual. God did not cause the car accident as punishment or part of some plan, but the accident was the result of random, unpredictable events. As result of the accident, God can take something tragic, and recreate it into an instrument of transformation. The person involved in the accident employed his or her free will and chose an alternative way of living based on a life-altering experience. The accident happened by chance which led to a conversion experience. Chance, then, can lead to human development in both the physical and spiritual realms. When chance is viewed in this way, chance clearly has its purpose. Chance and unpredictability are consistent with the purposes of God rather than working against it. When it comes to Chaos Theory, according to Doyne Farmer, physicist and one of the founders of Chaos Theory, chaos might provide "'an operational way to define free will.'" It could be a way to reconcile free will and determinism. "The system is deterministic, but you can't say [exactly] what it is going to do next"(Davis, 5).

Several essential questions must be considered. Is randomness in the world the essence of freedom? Is a spinning roulette wheel the exercising of free will? Can human choices and actions be placed in various categories of physics: Newtonian, quantum-mechanical, and chaos paradigms?

For Davis, in light of chaotic systems, there can no longer be a "clockwork universe." [God built the clock and set it into motion and walked away.] The universe is still governed by the laws in deterministic form, but there can be the amplification of small uncertainties. A thoroughly predictable universe as described the intellectuals of the Enlightenment is dead (Davis, 6). In reality the universe is not a simple, linear system. Davis cites the rotation of the planet Mars as an example of a chaotic element in the universe. Its axis is chaotic by wobbling between 0 and 60 degrees (Davis, 6-7).

An important function of Chaos Theory is to remind the theologian, the Church, and all people of faith that there are limitations to how much humanity can predict and seemingly control. Chaos Theory puts humanity in its place by humbling it. Christian fundamentalists want the world to be orderly and controlled. They want a Newtonian world where abortion is always wrong under any circumstance: A leads to B which results in C. C is bad and deserves punishment. The created order does not function that way. The world is chaotic, and the act of abortion—one's employment of free will for better or for worse—is just one more variable added to a very complex system. "Chaos Theory has demonstrated when the inherent limitations on human ability to predict and control the future. From a Christian perspective, such an encounter with the limits inherent in the nature of the physical realm, remind humanity of the fundamental distinction between an infinite Creator and a finite and limited creation, including humans. The new discoveries of Chaos Theory give man further reason to adopt a stance of 'epistemic humility' the face of a complex and unpredictable world" (Davis, 7). Simply, the Enlightenment and subsequent years that followed elevated humanity to such a level of arrogance that we became idolaters to our own egos, our own wealth, and our own power. Chaos Theory comes along and says you are at the mercy of something greater—unseen, unpredictable, and dangerous. The humbling experience comes when simple events suddenly give rise to very complex events, and this happens without prediction. Now, our ability to offer a complete picture of the physical world is drawn into question. If science now acknowledges the impossibility of predicting the future behavior of even a swinging pendulum, how can it possibly determine human behavior in linear fashion based on one's past and present actions, decisions, and environment? Charles Hodge (1797-1878), a Presbyterian theologian at Princeton, was surprisingly prophetic when it came to faith and science. Science's appeal is its ability to give a clear understanding of the world around us.

The Church is failing partially by its abandonment of orthodoxy coupled by its inability to take historic doctrines—Apostle's Creed and Nicene Creed— and recreate them in a language pertinent to the postmodern era. The worse thing to happen to Christianity, Hodge saw, was the denial of purpose and design in nature. For him, the denial of design in nature is a denial of God. The mainline Church has surrendered by incorporating scientific language [such as evolutionary and genetic language] into its own vocabulary, design and purpose. Why? The western Church has greater access to technology; thus, it puts its faith in handheld devices. Scientific explanations are now more acceptable than religious answers. Unfortunately, the wonder and awe of the universe as well as the poet's heart are forgotten in such a world. The Church is declining as a result. Third World churches are growing because they see design and purpose in nature from the lenses of faith. They have little to no access to technology. Once they do, unfortunately and ultimately, they will more than likely follow the path of the West. Other religions will follow suit with time.

In concurrence with theologian John Davis, the presence of chance and unpredictability does not remove purpose from the world. The instability brought on by chaotic systems can lead to new and creative emergences. Throughout the Bible, God works through people, and more times than not those people are very flawed who bring elements of chaos—Abraham lied about his wife, Moses murdered, and Peter denied. According to Aquinas, God is the first and foremost source or cause of all things and of all that happens: the death of a sparrow, the fall of governments, the rising of the sun, and the death and resurrection of Christ. God is the primary source, but God often works through secondary causes—people and natural laws.

Take the story of King David in 1 Samuel of the Old Testament. He is first described as the perfect candidate to serve as King of all Israel: "He sent and brought him in [before Samuel who is about to anoint him king].

Now he was ruddy and had beautiful eyes, and was handsome. The Lord said, 'Rise and anoint him, for this is the one'" (1 Samuel 16:12). King David was to bring order and stability to Israel. David sounds like the perfect candidate for today's political scene. However, there is an element of uncertainty from the beginning of David's kingship. David was the youngest of Jesse's sons. To anoint the youngest for such a position was virtually unheard of in the time of Samuel. Again, God chooses the least likely making a complex system even more complex. David rules Israel well—unifying the country, increasing its wealth, and expanding its borders like no other time. He was the apple of God's eye, and his kingship was moving forward. Then, an element of chaos is introduced to the system—Bathsheba. David, exercising his free will, chose not to lead his troops in battle like a good king should in the spring (see 2 Samuel 11). He chose to walk about on his roof, and by chance, he spotted a very beautiful woman named Bathsheba, "It *happened* [emphasis mine], late one afternoon, when David rose from his couch and was walking about on the roof of the king's house, that he saw from the roof a woman bathing; the woman was very beautiful" (2 Samuel 11:2). Bathsheba is the element of chance causing the proverbial train wreck. This chance encounter led to David's adultery [adultery is one of those chaotic elements tried to be controlled by the Ten Commandments], then to his lying, and ultimately to the murder of Uriah, Bathsheba's husband. As a result of this chaos, there is turbulence in the kingdom. However, David is transformed. He becomes a better king and remained God's chosen. This chance encounter with Bathsheba brought about the birth of Solomon who would go on to continue what his father started; he, too, will have chance encounters leading to chaos. Chaos increases with every new king of Israel.

Davis writes that there is a *logos* (Word) structure in God's created order which encompasses the "turbulent and unpredictable events studied by the chaos theorists." Chaos does not represent a "lawless or unbound chaos;" they are found in much deeper structures of order beyond what we see from the surface: "In the beginning was the Word, and the Word was with God … (John 1:1), and "The light shines in the darkness, and the darkness did not overcome it (John 1:5). Clearly, there is a much deeper structure communicated in the opening chapter of the Gospel of John than just light and dark (Davis, 9).

The Apostle Paul writes, "He (Christ) is the image of the invisible

God, the first-born of all creation; for in him all things in heaven and on earth were created, things visible and invisible. He himself is before all things, and in him all things hold together ..." (Colossians 1:15-17). This indicates that there is an underlying structure that holds the universe together while an element of chaos exists.

The Book of Job is perhaps the best example of how Chaos Theory and faith intersect. Job by the end of the book is lead by God through affliction after affliction [things completely out of his control] to the point where he receives a deeper awareness of the natural order and sometimes chaotic universe. This awareness can be a source of wonder and humility because God's creative handiwork becomes readily revealed. Chaos Theory may be the theological language of the 21st century, a new approach toward understanding both the limitations of human ability to control and to predict the future and the fullness or completeness of God's creative power. But what does this mean for the Church? It means the Church is given new words to describe the creeds and the orthodoxy of the early western and eastern churches; without surrendering meaning and purpose, the ancient creeds and liturgies can be translated into language relevant to the postmodern worshipper. .

Not only does Chaos Theory have theological implications that may shed some light on the free will and determinism debate, but it may also have something to say about Creation itself and the role of sin in the world in connection with free will. Sjord Bonting in his 1999 article, "Chaos Theory Revisited," states that Chaos Theory changes our view of the doctrine of *creatio ex nihilo* (creation out of nothing). Prior to creation, there was pre-existing water that represented, according to several places throughout scripture, chaos (Bonting, 1-3). That initial, unexplained Chaos was never eliminated during the act of creation, so a remnant or element of chaos was left behind. According to Genesis 1, " ...God swept over the face of the water," and God separated the waters, "Let there be a dome in the midst of the waters, and let it separate the waters from the waters." Waters, which represent chaos in the Bible, remain in Creation; only in prophetic texts does it say God will eliminate the seas. This chaos is sin in the world as best represented by images of the sea found throughout mainly the Old Testament and by the end of the New Testament. According to the New Testament Book of Revelation, the sea, i.e. chaos, is destroyed or abolished,

"Now I saw a new heaven and a new earth, for the first heaven and the first earth had passed away, and the sea was no more" (Revelation 21:1). Whereas we often consider the seas as a source of comfort and relaxation, ancient peoples considered the seas as chaotic. For them, the ocean represents turmoil, turbulence, and so forth. For Bonting, then, the remaining element of chaos that is part of Creation is the source of physical and moral evil. However, it should be added that God the Creator intentionally allowed the chaotic remnant of the primal seas to remain in Creation so that humanity could exercise its free will all the while working to eventually destroy it, thereby, returning the created world to a state of completion and perfection. An avenue for the exercise of free will had to be set loose so that humanity could have free will in order to choose God freely. Once God finally is satisfied with the state of Creation, God perfects it. It is all about free will, and chaos allows for that free will to be employed. Free will happens through chaos/sin serving as a medium. Chaos Theory answers the question of evil.

The more accurate [as opposed to the belief of God creating something from nothing] biblical view of creation involves the separation of the heavens and the earth from the dark and formless void, or the primordial, chaotic waters. From this void, God separated the primordial waters and creates just as a potter works with clay. Creation is not about *ex nihilo* [out of nothing], but rather it is about separation.

Bonting claims that the Hebrew word, "*bara*", used in Genesis is essential to understanding God's act of creation. This key word, as defined by Bonting, means separating, shaping into a form, defining, excluding and giving individuality, rather than, the calling forth from nothing. It is the English word, "create," that suggests *ex nihilo*, but this is not the Hebrew translation and/or understanding (Bonting, 2-5). In Genesis 1:2-10, God pushes back chaos in different acts of separation. The Genesis creation story tells of a God who continually creates in the world. Creation is an ongoing process; this ongoing act of creating occurs in large part to this remaining element of chaos that came from out of the primordial sea. Sin, which is the remnant also know as chaos, allows God to continually push forward toward a perfected Creation by eliminating chaos, so creation is continual. Creation has an ongoing history. In this view of historical creation, God renews and renews the face of the earth, "When you send forth your spirit; they are created; and you renew the face of the ground" (Psalm 104:30). The continual renewal looks toward the final creation of all things including all human institutions. God creates justice for those who have never known justice. God rises up the humble and the marginalized. God fulfills God's promises as revealed in history. However, through all this, the remnant of chaos continues to plague humanity. In Psalm 8, the "foes" or "enemy" mentioned represent the chaotic forces that God defeated, and yet paradoxically (for God is the God of paradox) God allows for a remnant of chaos to remain, while ordering these forces of chaos to fall under God's sovereignty. In a word, God has the authority to release or to hold back chaos. Human beings, God often chooses the weakest in society, are Creation's co-workers who are constantly threatened by the enemy, which is chaos or sin. Chaos imprisons all of creation, including humanity, until the final day when God destroys it. According to theologian Jurgen Moltmann, the Apostle Paul perceives the imprisoned nature as "yearning" and "sighing" for liberation. The mediators of Creation—Holy Spirit and the Word—wait and strive for the liberation of all things from that imprisonment brought about by chaos. Teilhard de Chardin incorporated the Theory of Evolution as the driving force toward perfection. Christ becomes *Christus Evoluter* or "the evolver Christ." This represents the creative side of redemption. The history of life and the cosmos is an evolution from simple to complex, a sort of Nietzsche's "Superman." Chardin also believed the incarnation of Christ should be understood as the beginning of a new phase in the evolution of life in general. Life gets better from the nativity forward. Moltmann said such an understanding fails to see the ambiguity in life. Evolution has victims. It has winners and losers, and the cruelty of life is felt by the weakest in society (Moltmann, 100-01). This is contrary to the biblical understanding of Christ's redefining human interaction and purpose of existence, "Whoever want to be first must be last of all and servant of all" (Mark 9:35), " ...and the last will be first" (Mark 10:31). In sum, redemption runs counter to evolution. Evolution gets turned upside down by Christ because Christ elevates the weak and marginalized in society. Evolution destroys them. It would be counter-intuitive to use an evolutionary model as a tool of God. Christians will often justify evolution as a device used by God to create the world, but in light of the risen Christ, this is not so. Christ is far from being the evolver. Christ is the redeemer of all things seen and unseen.

Chaos is an accurate way of describing sin in the world. Chaos is all around us. It is in the structure of an oak tree, a field of wild flowers, rivers and streams, and even our own bodies. Chaos is not intrinsic to these things, but rather, chaos externally acts upon a system. This chaotic presence can also be seen in things like economic cycles, terrorism, wildlife populations, and even family dynamics. Chaos, then, is externally present in many of the everyday systems we find ourselves in or around, and always unpredictable. Chaos lurks everywhere in random fashion. The conundrum is thus: humanity has free will but that free will is an illusion when taken into consideration with the greater reality of God's ultimate plan for the cosmos. The Archimedean Point supports that illusion because no matter where people place their metaphorical lever to leverage change in their lives, the fulcrum is always shifting, and the ground is shifting sand. Even though people have free will, all is vain and chasing after the wind.

Take a forge crew at a steel mill. The crew is running very efficiently, just as they were trained to do. Then, unexpectedly, the crew chief develops a drinking problem and another's marriage starts to collapse; the result is a decline in productivity. Alcoholism and marital problems are unforeseen to the crew chief. The plant manager cannot plan for such events. Alcoholism and a failing marriage introduced into the forging crew is equivalent to the introduction of sin or chaos bringing with it negative results. A simple night of alcohol consumption by one forklift driver could have disastrous consequences in the steel mill. Family members may have seen the alcoholism and failing marriage unfolding; whereas, the work place could not predict it. The forge crew chief has no way of predicting the factors that may increase or decrease production. Thus, each shift may operate smoothly and effectively, or each shift may not.

In regards to chaos, sin, and determinism, Neal Magee in his essay, "Determinism, Total Predictability and the Uncertainty Principal in Chaotic Systems: Theological Implications," outlines four theological points worth examining. First, following the act of creation, freedom is given to the entire universe to be co-creators with God while having to accept things like disease and natural disaster and moral evil brought about by humanity's choices. God does not desire sin in the world, but sin or chaos becomes the only way for human beings to freely act. It is the medium for free will. God does not will the actions of a killer, nor does God desire war, nor cancer, but God allows those things to be present in the world—just as God allowed an element of the original chaos to be released into the world. God has given the world the ability to be itself, to have its own system. This allows humanity to carry out free will. Second, God's actions within an unpredictable open system will always be unknown to humanity just as long-term weather forecasts cannot be 100 percent accurate. Thus, there is a natural, unexplained order to the universe which is known and yet unknown to people. Third, God is not one cause among many other causes in the universe. God is not the god of the gaps. The danger of understanding God as gap filler—God is used to explain that which is currently beyond human knowledge—is that as science begins to fill the gaps, God is methodically eliminated. And fourth, chaos theory provides the avenue for humans to exercise freewill which includes choosing good or evil/sin. As for determinism, the future is not some travel destination waiting for us to arrive. Our future is made—based on the exercising of our free will and the role of sin in the world—as we go a long; this is an eschatology based solely on free will (Magee, 6). Free will better describes the postmodern era as opposed to the ordered world of the Middle Age when everyone and everything had its place.

There are problems in seeing God's actions based on these four theological points. God does have a direct relationship with humanity— the God of Abraham, Isaac, and Jacob. Furthermore, through Christ, God stepped out of eternity and into human time. However, the potential for danger lies in how Magee's model could be construed as one limiting God. However, free will drives human history while God predetermines the much larger picture. Theological positions are taken concerning how God does not know the outcome of humanity's free actions because of a free and independent will. This, however, is problematic and restrains God, but the issue can be addressed by simply saying God in fact knows the outcomes but chooses not to share them with His Creation; thus, humanity can act freely in the world believing the future is not yet set.

Thus, chaos theory is a fitting, viable scientific theory to use in connection for explaining pain and moral evil in the world as well as free will and God's continuing creative hand in human history. This is where religion and science have common ground: to come to the table for debate knowing full well the two have inherent conflicts. The conflicts are of an amiable nature. The conflict is the remnant of that chaotic, primordial sea which God tames and allows to effect human affairs just as God gave permission to Satan to test Job. If there is no absolute free will, then why should God bother to continually create and push Creation forward towards completion or wholeness? Bonting points out that God assigned boundaries to the primal sea in Job 38:8—11, [God says to Job concerning God's own creative power] "' ... who shut in the sea with doors when it burst out from the womb?—when I made the clouds its garment, and thick darkness its swaddling band, and prescribed bounds for it, and set bars and doors, and said, Thus far shall you come, and no farther, and here shall your proud waves be stopped?" Also in other parts of scripture, God sets guard over the sea or the original chaos. God also commands the water back, as described in Psalm 18:15, "Then the channels of the sea were seen, and the foundations of the world were laid bare at your rebuke, O Lord, at the blast of the breadth of your nostrils." Even the Psalmist acknowledges a creation by separation rather than from out of nothing, *ex nihilo*. The raging sea is ordered back by God [remember, God allows a remnant to slip through the cracks to provide an avenue for free will] in the prophetic book of Nahum: "He rebukes the sea and makes it dry, and he dries up all the rivers ..." (Nahum 1:4). God begins to destroy chaos, and finally, in the Book of Revelation 21:1, God destroys all the remnant of chaos, and Creation is perfected: " ...and the sea was no more" (Bonting, 1). Chaos is abolished resulting in a state of wholeness and perfection. In sum, Creation is not yet complete because God allowed a fraction of that original, primordial sea [chaos] to plague humanity while allowing humanity to exercise free will. God works in creation by holding back that remaining element while allowing some to slip through thereby shaping humanity until it no longer succumbs to chaos, bringing Creation closer and closer to fulfillment until one day all of Creation is completed or made whole. This will come about by one final act of creating, "Then I saw a new heaven and a new earth ..." (Revelation 21:1). What makes this Creation different from the last? Revelation 21:1 continues, " …the first earth had passed away, and the *sea was no more* [emphasis mine]. Finally, the question must be asked: Where did the initial, primal sea of chaos come from? There is no answer. This question is unanswerable. That is the divine mystery. Revelation concerns the destruction of chaos and the creation of perfection and order. Genesis identifies chaos' presence, and Revelation eliminates it.

The current understanding of Creation as being *ex nihilo* has many holes in it. It was used in the Second Century to counter the teachings of Marcion and the other Gnostic groups. From there, creation out of nothing, *ex nihilo,* was passed from church leader to church leader until finally becoming a doctrine of the Church. Creation from nothing eliminates all mystery, and everything gets wrapped up in a neat, little package.

Bonting states that there are conceptual, biblical, scientific, and theological problems with the *ex nihilo.* The concept is too elusive because no one can picture absolute nothingness. Thus, why would the Creation Story in the Book of Genesis communicate by oral tradition to uneducated people concepts that are unfathomable to its audience? What human being can contemplate absolute nothingness? Karl Barth tries to reconcile some of the differences by treating the primordial sea as an existing nothingness (*nihil ontologicum*); in other words, it is simply a metaphysical statement. Biblically, it is difficult to make a case for *creatio ex nihilo.* Time and time again we see examples throughout the Old Testament of how God held back or guarded the remaining primordial waters with the sovereignty to release it when God chooses. God still holds back. It is a theme scattered throughout scriptures. This is not the case with *creatio ex nihilo.* The only place where it might appear is in the first chapter of Genesis, but afterwards, it does not show up any where else. The origin of matter is not answered, " …in the presence of the God in whom he believed, who gives life to the dead and calls into existence the things that do not exist" (Romans 4:17). The origin of matter is unimportant because it is not an issue relevant to the every day lives of people. Matter just "is" and nothing else needs to be said. [Science, too, wrestles with the nature of matter, especially in light of new theories put forward by theoretical sciences.] Matter was not present at the beginning; only formless void was there, so the void became the clay to be shaped by God. From a scientific point of view, creation out of nothingness makes little sense because nothing comes out of nothing; and theologically, explaining cosmic beginnings from nothing is as perplexing for the theologian as it is for the scientist, poet, and philosopher. Bonting says, "Explaining a cosmic origin from true *nihil* [nothing] causes theologians as much of a problem as it does scientists. Karl Barth (1960) tries to reconcile the initial chaos of Genesis 1:2 with 'nothing' by assuming a *nihil privatium,* which he calls '*das Nichtige*' a 'nothing' of things already existing, but not real before they were created; however, this is not really different from an initial chaos," (Bonting, 1-2).

Finally, chaos theory when tied to the question of creation also addresses the problem of evil; chaos theory can be considered as theodicacy. *Creatio ex nihilo* makes God responsible for evil in the world. Origen tried to solve this with the doctrine of original sin (Bonting, 2). With the remnant of chaos in the world leftover from the primordial seas described in Genesis 1:2, God is now seen as a god who is involved in the world through continual creation. This ongoing act of creation involves God holding back chaos while moving all of Creation toward complete and perfect state. "I retain the idea of creation from initial chaos with a continuing creation and a remaining element of chaos that God will abolish on the last day. I then propose that this remaining element of chaos is the source of evil in our world" (Bonting, 3). Clearly, *creatio ex nihilo* is not biblical, and unlike Gnostic dualism, the application of chaos theory maintains the absolute authority of God because only God can hold back the primordial waters. Furthermore, God battles the remaining chaos in the world, and as Bonting writes, this does not diminish God's omnipotence; in fact, this makes God greater than a creator who allows initial creation to be spoiled by Original Sin. It also allows for a god to be active in the world and not a cosmic watch maker. Again, God let out some remnant of chaos, as represented by the waters in which God divided, so that humans can act freely and make choices. This is essential for demonstrating God's sovereignty. Even the power of chaos is under God's command. The Uncertainty Principle, as described in chapter 2, put a crack in the scientific wall of determinism and allowed theology to enter into the discussion of a deterministic world, and theology can push beyond that debate because the uncertainty principle brought an end to a completely deterministic world, and theology adds there will be a time when chaos is eliminated. For the theologian, chaos must take on a greater presence.

In summation, Creation stood as a system. Humanity was added to that system making it more complex, and then, the serpent, which is one of the symbols of chaos, introduced the possibility for chaos into this perfect system. Adam and Eve exercise their free will, and thus, we have chaos, i.e. sin, let loose in the world and always lurking in the shadows. Chaos provided the mechanism or medium for Adam and Eve to act freely in the world, and they chose wrong.

Genesis 3:17-18 states that God informs Adam, "Because ... you ate from the tree which I had forbidden you to eat, cursed be the soil because of you! ... It will yield you thorns and thistles, as you eat the produce of the land." Here, we are given an example of how chaos works. We see the introduction of chaos into agriculture. Farmers cannot predict when the growing season will have ample rain or not, or if it will be a cool or hot summer, or how many thorns and thistles will sprout in the soy bean field. Life was a simple system for Adam and Eve; then, it became complex when the two realized they were naked.

Paul probably had Genesis 3 in mind when he wrote Romans 8:19 through 25. It was a common belief among Paul's Jewish peers that when Adam disobeyed God's command and subsequently fell into captivity to sin and death; this is extended to the entire universe. Not only did men and women suffer for taking it upon themselves to sin, but all of Creation has suffered for it and stands in the need of redemption, or the elimination of chaos. And what is redemption? For nature, it is a return to that state of perfection prior to Adam's guilt, a time when chaos was not present.

Nature is restlessly waiting for fulfillment and meaning and completion. Creation longs to once again be unified, for Paul writes "We know that the whole creation has been groaning in labor pains until now; and not only the creation, but we ourselves groan ..." (Romans 8:22). Nature is isolated from that perfect relationship with God and humans, and it finds itself in an unpredictable universe. Out of nature's loneliness it groans and moans; the wind wails; the seas sigh.

Again, Paul tells us we already have the first fruits or the first installment of the Spirit that came at Pentecost, and now we are waiting for the redemption of our bodies, or in other words, that last installment of the Spirit which makes us complete and whole, the elimination of chaos. Pentecost was another act of Creation pushing the universe toward perfection and completion: "And suddenly from heaven there came sound like the rush of a violent wind, and it filled the entire house where they were sitting. Divided tongues, as of fire, appeared among them, and a tongue rested on each of them. ..And at this sound the crowd gathered and was bewildered, because each one heard them speaking in the native language of each" (Acts 2:1-8). In other words, we see God bringing order to chaos—from many tongues to one tongue: complexity to simplicity.

The general idea Paul is communicating is that since we have hope through the first fruits or first installment of the Spirit at Pentecost, we come to expect that something far greater than anything we have ever known is waiting for us. And like nature, we too groan inwardly and wait for that restoration. The Second Letter of Peter tells us to wait patiently for this restored relationship, a new heaven and a new earth, for it is there where righteousness shall dwell, a perfect state without chaos.

The Church must ask itself what is its place in this movement toward perfection and develop a new paradigm that holds together nature and Spirit in a unified and integrated way. If we look at Christ's resurrection from this perspective, we can move from a human-history Christology to a new, ecological, all-inclusive Christology. There can be no human final redemption until the entire universe, including the natural order, is redeemed. God will provide. Amid the chaos, God offers stability and life, and the future belongs to God. God is not an encyclopedia that one opens to find the answers to life. God is the Alpha and the Omega. God simply "is." God is beyond hypothesis and observation.

Columnist for the *Seattle Post-Intelligencer* writes these words, "So why does the conflict between religion and science rage on? Misunderstanding and exaggerated claims for either science or religion by their more zealous proponents is one explanation. Another is what's at the root of many, perhaps most, of our world's conflicts: fear and the lust for power. Religion has a word for that, "sin." And that is one religious doctrine, perhaps the only one, which is empirically, that is to say scientifically, verifiable" (Robinson, 2). The Church reminds science that people are imperfect; thus, science is imperfect.

We live in truly a remarkable and unique era. Science and technology are firmly rooted in the world, but what about the Church? Is it equally rooted in the world? The question remaining unanswered is, has the Church or has religion, in general found its place in an ever-increasing, scientific world? The answer lies in the relationship between religion and science. Any attempt to reconcile the two would be a mistake because when one combines the influence of technology with an ever increasing secularization of society, church/religion loses. Science limits the creativity of God. Science, through technology, makes religion, especially the Church, irrelevant or meaningless to generations who now find community in cyber space through chat rooms, text messaging, and *myspace.com*. Churches are incarnate. The Church is about real, flesh and blood community. The celebration of the Eucharist defines the Church and sets it apart from the rest of the world. Science cannot capture the beauty and essence of the Eucharist. One cannot taste the bread and wine without being in community.

Church and science/technology serves humanity and each other best when the two remain in conflict, pushing and pulling against one another. This conflict does not need to be a battle in which a winner emerges. Instead, the conflict can be a friendly one which improves the lives of humanity. However, there must be some common ground in order for the two to come together. That common ground may be the theoretical sciences such as Chaos Theory.

For the Church, it is about relevancy in the 21st century. The more it engages the same debates, like the Creation vs. Evolution debate or the abortion debate, the more irrelevant Church and religion become, and so instead, science must be called upon by the Church to explain all moral and ethical reasons for technological advancements: How does this help or hinder humanity? Finally, some real issues facing humanity is its stature or position in the universe, and providing purpose, meaning, and human connection to a world that seem disconnected. The Church must provide meaning and purpose to people's lives; if not, humanity is swept up in technology, and the Church as known today will be no more. Community means survival and growth.

Chapter 5: The Mystic Rhythm

The finest emotion of which we are capable is the mystic emotion. Herein lies the germ of all art and all true science. Anyone to whom this feeling is alien, who is no longer capable of wonderment and lives in a state of fear is a dead man. To know that what is impenetrable for us really exists and manifests itself as the highest wisdom and the most radiant beauty, whose gross forms alone are intelligible to our poor faculties—this knowledge, this feeling ... that is the core of the true religious sentiment. In this sense, and in this sense alone, I rank myself among profoundly religious men"
(Albert Einstein).

The "Old Man and The Bear," a short story by southern fiction writer William Faulkner, tells a tale of the disappearance of certain clarity to life, an innate innocence struggling against an increasingly evil and disintegrating society. The plot of the story hinges on a seemingly mythological bear. The bear and its natural surroundings represent a primordial innocence as well as reflecting a mystical element to life.

Year after year a group of men come together as a community to hunt the mythological bear. It is the seasonal cycle of the hunt, and the liturgy of the attempted kill that brings the hunters together. The myth of the bear holds the community together.

"The Bear" spans a period from 1877 to 1888, during a time when the young hunter, Ike, grows from a boy to a twenty-one year-old man, a movement from the innocence of childhood to the jadedness of adulthood. Faulkner gives the bear such mythological qualities as wisdom and dignity; it is a seemingly unbeatable adversary—a god-like foe squaring off against the hunters. The animal is taintless and beautiful but corruptible as in the Garden of Eden prior to the Fall; the bear roams freely through the forest unfettered by constraints. It epitomizes free will, and yet, humanity seeks to destroy its freedom.

Faulkner progressively describes the woods as being chewed away by humanity as if bite by bite the myth is destroyed leaving emptiness, a dark void of nothingness. Science is the myth destroyer. In its lust to explain or answer the questions of life, humanity's collective soul is gnawed away. The myths that bond humanity are weakened, and the tapestry that tells the human story through its myths begins to unravel. Then, in the story, when the hunter, Boon, and the dog, Lion, kill the bear it collapses under its own weight and subsequently and thunderously falls to the ground ending an era while ushering in the modern, scientific\technological age. The myth has been destroyed, and the human story is no more. The destruction of some myths is important, such as myths that cause harm, objectify, and dehumanize. During the middle ages, the world was believed to be flat, and other erroneous beliefs about the world prevailed. When science became free from its religious constraints and entered into conflict with the Church, scientists used human reason to discover key truths about the universe as with Galileo. Such scientific discovery revealed that the world is far more complex, thus, showing the creative power of God. Humanity has the intellectual capacity to impact—for good or for bad—the world. Science, devoid of military and greed, changes the world for the better by improving the quality of life, and the Church helps people find meaning in the world.

In the not too distant future, technology will be available to allow us to choose our genes. Parents will be given the opportunities to make choices about what particular genetic traits they were like to see in their children. This is similar to the baby factories of Nazis Germany when men and women were chosen by their characteristics to produce babies with particular genetic traits through selective breeding. This parental genetic selection is called, *Germinal Choice Technology* that allows parents to influence the genetic make up of their children at the point of conception. The next step in this technology is to alter the sperm and egg in order to derive a particular child. The initial goal of *Germinal Choice Technology* is to prevent diseases before they strike. The goal is noble, but such technologies begin to unravel the human story. The stature of humanity is reduced to test tubes in a laboratory, and the human struggle, which defines who we are, is lessened; the struggle of hunting the bear all those years bonded a group of multi-generational hunters. Once the bear was killed, the bonds were broken. Their culture became extinct.

Certain members of the deaf community strongly opposes the use of cochlear implants technology because it diminishes the deaf culture and treats deafness as some thing inferior to the general population. Similarly, "Some people worry about a loss of diversity, but I think a more wrenching issue may be parents who decide to specifically select an embryo that would result in a child with a serious health condition. Should parents be allowed to make such choices?" (Stock, 19) What if the parents make a mistake or the laboratory technician makes the mistake? People are human. Science has yet to find a perfection gene. If a mistake is made, are the parents willing to live with the consequences, or will they terminate babies until they get the one they want?

What defines culture is its diversity. Diversity is part of the human story because it challenges us to be in community together despite differences. Diversity challenges humanity to care for the weak and marginalized, and it makes humanity better.

The culture of the Church, like the pristine forest in Faulkner's "Old Man and the Bear," is now violated by the postmodern, scientific, technologically-driven age. One day, will we be able to honestly tell our children that God—whether one fully believes or not—made you very special and unique? Are we facing the height of human arrogance when we can now tell our children, "Your mommy and daddy made you by selecting the best of our genetic characteristics?" The western Church is the caretaker of the human story or myth. Destroy the myth, and you destroy the people. When myths are challenged and unveiled, a part of humanity dies. Science seeks to give logical explanations for the myths that give humanity meaning and purpose. In regards to research and in order to remain objective, people are no more than an acid called DNA. Several cable television programs are now devoted to explaining or explaining away—either one is just as dangerous—the stories of the Bible, such as the Hebrews crossing of the Red Sea or Noah's Arc. For Jews and Christians, an explanation of how it happened is basically irrelevant. The fact that the story and its meaning has been passed down for thousands of years is what gives it relevance. The tapestry of stories holding humanity together is now unraveling due to the pull of science away from being human in an existential way. Stories of the people and the belief systems are what hold humanity together. The mystery of life creates a universal bond that transcends nations, cultures, races, ethnicity, and gender even though at times the mystery often clashes with other mysteries. Just as the death of the bear brought about the demise of innocence, science at times threatens who we are as a people. One role the Church must fully employ is to communicate or remind people who they are in the world especially in the midst of a synthetic and sometimes chaotic and ever-changing world. World religions must eventually communicate to people that they are more than DNA in a dish. This will help give the Church relevancy in the 21st century. Why is communicating and reinforcing who one is so important? *The Futurist* magazine predicts that by the year 2017 machine knowledge exceeds human knowledge, and by 2030 robots become physically and mentally superior to humans (*The Futurist*, 35-36). Thus, the only thing that will separate people from robot is spirit because bio-mechanical flesh will follow. Thus, another role to keep the church relevant in the future involves proclaiming the following message, "Yet you have made them a little lower than God, and crowned them with glory and honor. You have given them dominion over the works of your hands; you have put all things under their feet, all sheep and oxen, and also the beasts of the field, the birds of the air, and the fish of the sea, whatever passes along the paths of the seas," (Psalm 8:5-8).

Science cannot encroach on spirit nor can it explain it away unless people of faith allowed it to happen. Religion can be the candle light of hope in a world where humanity is left trying to figure out what it means to be human. Again, without myth, humanity is lost; it has no roots or sense of direction. By its very nature, albeit morally neutral, science destroys myths in its attempt to explain all things. This destruction is a byproduct of what started out as an altruistic act. As with the shifting fulcrum, science must move from one explanation to one another, but in doing so, it destroys the myths along the way. This is why any attempt to merge science and religion is extremely dangerous. The Church is the keeper of the myth and weaver of tapestries by telling an existential story of why we are here and not how we got here. The "why" is more important than the "how." There must be an amiable conflict between religion and science so that science has boundaries and is made aware of the need for myth, and the Church is better informed or educated on the nature of the universe in order to have a different appreciation for Creation. Science is not concerned with the individual and collective narratives of people, and how, like threads in a tapestry, people's lives overlap and intersect. This is one of several important roles for the Church. The Church cares for one's narrative as well as the collective narrative of humanity, and how that narrative intertwines with the biblical narrative weaving a moral, ethical, and existential tapestry.

Humanity cries out for the mythical and the mystical. Thus, these two essential components for what it means to be human must be retained in the 21st century even as science advances which is inevitable. Furthermore, these two components cannot be passed down by text messaging or emailing. Mythical and mystical are passed along by shared experience in a real, authentic way. This means one must belong to a community where flesh and blood meet.

Because part of the role of the Church is to preserve the story, a level of orthodoxy is essential for understanding God as revealed in scripture and revelation. The Church must figure out what it is in relation to modernity. This includes the ancient creeds and liturgies that provide a sense of stability in an ever-changing world. Not carrying out this role, the Church stands in danger of being meaningless in a world of genetics and nano-bytes. The Church must refocus itself by moving away from the notion that the Creation story is a literal account of how humans got here toward an understanding of why we are here, and then communicate that understanding. The how-we-got-here debate fails for the Church when encountering science. When it comes to the existential question of why we are here, science is unable to provide a comforting answer for humanity. This means stories like that of Adam and Eve must be understood for what they are—a myth that points toward a greater understanding of who we are. Literalism serves no purpose here, for it does not point to something greater. For example, the healing stories of Jesus are not about this guy walking around healing people here and there. When taken literally, Jesus is simply a physician, but when read through mythological lenses Jesus' healing encounters describe a greater understanding of human existence as well as something bigger than the individual. For Christians, then, that "something bigger" is a time when chaos is gone and the kingdom of God is ushered into the world. Disease is chaos. When people are suffering, the words of science provide little comfort. The Church, on the other hand, provides the light to help lead people through the darkness.

As stated previously, one reason the Church has had difficulties providing this leadership is that, unlike science, it does not build upon the knowledge of the past. In other words, the story of Adam and Eve is not given 21st century language and meaning. Many people of faith want to "preserve" scripture or freeze it in time. Believers fail to realize that the Bible is a living document and must be adapted for every generation. What is needed is orthodoxy without dogma. Orthodoxy with dogma keeps it from being reinvented, and keeps the Church from recognizing freshness, renewal, and reformation. Again, orthodoxy provides the foundation in which faith is built upon, just as science builds upon previous discovery. Without the dogma but with the orthodoxy, humanity can receive by revelation relevant attributes of God fresh for the 21st century and yet remaining biblically based. God did not stop creating in the Book of Acts, when God formed the Church. If the Church does not keep its eyes, ears, soul, and heart wide open to receive 21st century revelation, it runs the risk of irrelevancy. A theological language for the 21st century must be found in order for the Church to be a meaningful part and even a central part of people's lives. Foundational understandings of God—creator, redeemer, sustainer— can remain unchanged, but how God acts in the world or how God is present in the world or how God is revealed in the world is as numerous as the stars. God's actions in the 21ˢᵗ century are far different than the 18ᵗʰ century. One possible, fresh, and relevant way of understanding how God acts and is known in the world is "The Mystic Rhythm," an expression borrowed from the music rock group, "Rush." This is a new myth for a new era.

John Updike perhaps said it best, "That the joy of creation, flowing through the generations of birds and bacteria, human beings and arboreal titans as they rise and fall, is not an illusion but an eternal bliss …" (*Toward the End of Time*, 232).

The Genesis account of creation makes it clear that Creation was shaped from primordial waters through the Divine, spoken word (Genesis 1:3). God spoke the world into being. That spoken word involves vibration. All one has to do is place his or her hand on the throat and speak. Vibrations are easily felt. The vibration of the Spirit of God permeates creation like a choir or instrument. Often, the cosmic song is heard like violins playing in the background at a social gathering. Sometimes we hear it, and sometimes we do not, but the song goes on for eternity. A common understanding of Genesis 1:2 is that God moved across the face of the waters and created the universe from nothing. In the opening of Genesis the Hebrew word, *ruach,* is often translated as Spirit. Jurgen Moltmann understands it, and rightfully so, as this, "The Hebrew word *ruach* is often translated Spirit, as it is here; but a better translation is 'wind' or 'breath'. The Hebrew word *rahaph* is generally rendered as 'hover' or 'brood.' But according to Deuteronomy 32:11 ["As an eagle stirs up its nest, and hovers over its young; as it spreads its wings, takes them up"] and Jeremiah 23:9 ["my heart is crushed within me, all my bones shake … because of the Lord and because of his holy words], it really means vibrating, quivering, moving, and exciting. If this is correct, then we shouldn't just think of the image of a fluttering or brooding dove. We should think of the fundamental resonances of music out of which sounds and rhythms emerge" (Moltmann, 96). What is interesting about this understanding of Creation is its closeness to string theory as described by author Brian Green in his book, *The Elegant Universe*. Matter is composed of atoms which in turn are made of quarks and electrons. According to string theory, all such particles are actually made of tiny, looped strings that vibrate like a violin. In

Genesis 1 the Spirit of God hovered over the face of the waters. Closely related to Moltmann's understanding, Green uses the language of theoretical science whereas Moltmann thinks theologically, "With the discovery of superstring theory, musical metaphors take on a startling reality, for the theory suggests that the microscopic landscape is suffused with tiny strings whose vibrational patterns orchestrate the evolution of the cosmos" (Green, 135). It is here where 21st century theoretical sciences contribute to a relevant understanding of God. Moltmann would argue that the vibration orchestrates ongoing creation activity. Ezekiel 37:1-14 describes this orchestra of heavenly music. Ezekiel is taken up in a vision, and he was set down in the middle of a valley surrounded by dry bones. Of course, the bones represent Israel in exile; Israel as a nation is practically dead. The Lord asks Ezekiel if he believes the bones can come to life, i.e. can life be given to the Israelites? Can there be re-creation? Ezekiel gives God a very vague answer—"O Lord, God, you know." Next, God tells Ezekiel to "Prophesy to these bones, and say to them: 'O dry bones, hear the word of the Lord.' Thus says the Lord God to these bones: 'I will cause breath to enter you, and you shall live.'" Here, the breath is the same wind or spirit that can be found in the Genesis account of creation. Then, God tells Ezekiel how sinews, flesh, skin, and breathe will come upon these bones. Ezekiel does what God asks and prophesied to the bones, "…suddenly there was a noise, a rattling and the bones came together…." In other words, renewal, re-creation is happening here in order to provide hope to Israel by showing how God will act in a different way, but all this is preceded by vibration, a mystical song. The improbable will suddenly be probable. God introduces an alternative reality. What is important for this discussion is that when the breath of creation comes upon the bones, the bones begin to vibrate, rattle, shake, and make a noise. The mystic rhythm pulsates through the lifeless, dry bones. Then, there is life where there once was none.

String theory, according to Green, resolves any conflict between general relativity and quantum mechanics. It has yet to be empirically proven. If true, it is a truly unified theory because all things are derived from one basic element—vibrating strings. People of faith can call those vibrating strings the song of God. The song is not God, but merely an attribute of the eternal, Divine. Because these vibrating strings are the smallest of anything and everything, they represent the end of the end—all things begin here just as all things begin with God. Is this God's signature on Creation? As stated in a previous chapter, theoretical sciences stand the best chance of working with theology while maintaining a certain level of conflict because even though there are some similarities between religion and theoretical sciences, there remains many differences that cannot be reconciled and should not be reconciled. According to Green, the string is fundamental. The violin model is used by Green to describe the quantum, vibrating strings. Each violin string has its own pattern of vibration known as resonances. Each string, in theory, has very similar qualities or properties. The string can support resonant vibrational patterns because of its evenly spaced peaks and troughs "exactly fitting along its spatial extent." A violin's vibrational patterns create notes giving rise to music. Green's theory states that different strings give rise to mass and force changes (Green, 142-43).

By linking vibration/song to Creation, we are given a very beautiful image of God and of Creation. The entire universe plays its tune, and that song sung by a heavenly choir can be heard in the beating of a human heart and the fluttering of bird wings. The Creator is the source of all life. God can be felt and experienced if we only listen, and be still and know that God is God. We are part of a cosmic dance; however, chaos can disrupt the dance. Now, when we begin to think about how Creation was sung into existence, our ears must be opened in order to hear the song of God. "In the quickening breath and through the form-giving word, the Creator sings out his creatures in the sounds and rhythms in which he has his joy and his good pleasure. That is why there is something like a *cosmic liturgy* and a music of the spheres" (Moltmann, 96). Creation is not a one time event. The song continues to unfold—an opera, a Broadway musical, a choir, all without end.

This creative, cosmic song or cosmic vibration is found in the Earth, right under our feet. Scientists first discovered what they call "Earth's Hum" about a decade ago. This hum occurs far below the threshold of human hearing. The earth is drumming a constant, ethereal, mystical rhythm. Constant notes of varying vibrations are every where on the planet from oceans to mountains to winds and trees. Earth is God's great symphony; Christ is the director, and the Holy Spirit provides the sound. The daily release of energy required to generate the earth's song is that of a large earthquake. Columnist Mark Morford of the SF Gate likens it appropriately to a "giant Tibetan singing bowl, flicked by God's middle finger and set to a mesmerizing, low ring for about ten billion years ..." (Morford, 2). The entire planet sings out its song, a song of creation, energy, and mystery. Humanity, too, is part of that song.

Morford writes on how human beings adore song and music and tone and rhythm. We hear a favorite hymn—perhaps one sung at a loved one's funeral—and we quiver with emotion. A favorite song is on the radio, and we tear up. Perhaps, music brings us closer to the Divine than anything else. The entire planet sings God's praises. Morford describes it this way: "Somewhere, somehow, deep in your very cells and bones and DNA, it links you back to the source, to the Earth's own vibration, the pulse of the cosmos" (Morford, 3). This pulse is the very life force of God; this vibration, this song that is in our very being and seemingly in all of creation is God's fingerprint.

Researchers are not sure what cause earth's song which makes Morford's description of it so fitting because it is mysterious. It was first believed that the "hum" originated below the surface of the earth—areas of rock moving up and down. Recently, ring-like oscillations caused by the interactions of several different phenomena might be responsible for creating the "hum." Also, investigators think that perhaps this song originates from the churning ocean or maybe the rolling atmosphere. In a word, earth's hum is a mystery; unfortunately, in its need to know, science struggles to kill the mystery. Clearly, based on available research, earth's song illustrates the inter-connectedness of all things. Are all things tuned by one Creator?

The mystic rhythm unifies nature and the divine that has been divided since the Enlightenment. Every human breath, every pulse from humans to animals, every sound pattern of footsteps on a rain-soaked sidewalk, every purr of cat or bark of a dog, and so on has rhythm; this will unify all things because all things have rhythm. When there is a pulse out of rhythm, there you find chaos in the form of a heart attack.

Both the Old and New Testaments are musical—from the Song of Moses in Exodus 15 to the Psalmists declaration in Psalm 33:3 to praise with lyre and harp and to sing a new song and to Revelation 14:3 where the harpists play and the 144,000 sing a new song before the throne. Many of the New Testament references to music are directly connected to an eschatological (end times) expectation when God destroys chaos and the world is perfected in complete harmony. . Take Paul's letter to the Ephesians 5:19: " …but be filled with the Spirit, as you sing psalms and hymns and spiritual songs among yourselves, singing and making melody to the Lord in your hearts …" Make melody because God is the song just as God is love. In Ephesians 5, verses 15 through 17 Paul offers up a warning that the days are numbered, the end is coming: "Be careful then how you live, not as unwise people but as wise, making the most of the time, because the days are evil." So, within this context of the eschatological expectation, the people of faith are called to sing Psalms, hymns, and spiritual songs. Music is what reconnects humanity to God and to one another. The very breath of life, the Spirit in which God sung creation into being, enters into the hearts of the Ephesians, and they join in that same song with the expectation of the beginnings of a new creation that is both here but not yet. The Spirit enters the heart. The people join in the song praising God's handiwork. Praise and thanksgiving in the form of song are faithful responses to what God has done and will do. How fitting to praise the God who sung creation into being through song and hymns. Music joins the natural rhythm of the heart and of the Earth. Paul uses similar words in Colossians 3:16 which describe the song of the heart as an appropriate praise of God. When you get to the Book of Revelation, the so-called end of the times book, creation is finally perfected and yet the songs remain. The world, much to the dismay of those who read Revelation literally, does not end. Chaos ends. The world is renewed. The Lamb takes the book from the "right hand of the One who was seated on the throne" (Rev. 5:7). This is immediately followed by a crescendo of three hymns sung in praise of the Lamb. The worship and songs of praise on earth rise up to join the heavenly worship or the song of God. The voice of many angels, living creatures, and the elders—"myriads of myriads and thousands and thousands"—join the heavenly choir (Rev. 5:11). What we have is a cosmic harmony of heaven and earth, including the animals. Both heaven and earth are locked in a dance and singing praises to the Lamb who will restore creation to perfection, "Then I heard every creature in heaven and on earth and under the earth and in the sea, and all that is in them, singing …" (Revelation 5:13). The song comes from outside and into the human heart. Clearly, every living thing on earth has a song to sing, a mystic rhythm resides in all of life in order to sing praises to the One who sits on the throne and to the Lamb. The mystic rhythm is a spider's web. When a strand is plucked, all of Creation can feel it. With the appearance of the Lamb in Revelation chapter 14, song breaks out. Furthermore, the writer of Revelation combines very elemental sounds—water and thunder—with an instrument and choir to announce the coming of the Lamb, "And I heard a voice from heaven like the sound of many waters and like the sound of loud thunder; the voice I heard was like the sound of harpists playing on their harps, and they sing a new song before the throne …" (Rev. 14:2-3).

With this musical backdrop, the Lamb stands on Mount Zion with a choir of 144,000, who sing a new song, to face the Dragon, the beast from the sea and the beast from the earth. In other words, the pattern and orderliness of music challenges the chaos of the primordial waters. Notice, neither weapons of war nor armies are used to face the enemy. A new song sung by a choir and by the Lamb, whose voice sounds like a harp, faces down the beasts. We are given yet another song of praise in the fifteenth chapter of Revelation. The setting is a "sea of glass mixed with fire." Standing next to the sea is the heavenly host holding harps of God in their hands. Again, the sea, which represents chaos, is challenged by the weapon of music. Remember, the biblical understanding of sea is that it represents chaos. Chaos has been destroyed as part of God's plan for perfection. More interesting, the conquerors of the beasts hold "harps of God in their hands," a direct connection to this musical quality of God. And here, "they sing the Song of Moses, the servant of God, and the song of the Lamb" (Rev. 15:3); the Song of Moses comes from Exodus 15:1-18 and Deuteronomy 31:30-32:43. The Song of the Lamb and the Song of Moses are not the same because the Song of Moses represents the old song God used to create, and the new Song of the Lamb represents the new creation, a perfected world. There still remains a mystic rhythm of song and instrument and choir which connects and transitions the old creation to the new creation. The songs here in Revelation 14:2-4 clearly are songs of victory or the elimination of chaos. Chaos is finally defeated. Christ in the Book of

Revelation is strictly depicted as the one with a rod of iron. However, how interesting it would be to think of the Prince of Peace standing before the beast of chaos with a lyre in his arms.

If we go back to the Old Testament, especially the prophet Isaiah, we are given the same sense that all of creation sings in harmony with the One who sung it into being. Isaiah 42:10 talks about a new song, "Sing to the Lord a new song, his praise from the end of the earth! Let the sea roar and all that fills it, the coastlands and their inhabitants. Let the desert and its towns lift up their voice" (Isaiah 42:10). Here, it is clear that the entire world is to sing in unity the same song in perfect harmony. The sea roars aloud, as well as all the creatures and plants that fill the earth, and sings its song of praise. The prophet Isaiah also describes how all kinds of people from all kinds of places sing together in one voice the praises of God. In Isaiah 55:12, the choir is expanded to include mountains, hills, and trees, "For you shall go out in joy, and be led back in peace; the mountains and the hills before you shall burst into song, and all the trees of the field shall clap their hands. Instead of the thorn shall come up the cypress; instead of the brier shall come up the myrtle; and it shall be to the Lord for a memorial, for an everlasting sign that shall not be cut off." Not only is humanity being heard, but now the trees are clapping which also provides a wonderful image of trees swaying in the wind, the breath of God. The prophet tells us, "They lift up their voices, they sing for joy; they shout from the west over the majesty of the Lord. Therefore in the east give glory to the Lord; in the coastlands of the sea glorify the name of the Lord, the God of Israel. From the ends of the earth we hear songs of praise of glory to the Righteous One, and yet, even in times of despair, the cosmic beat goes on. Isaiah 16 describes how joy and gladness have been taken away and how the land no longer yields; the vineyards no longer sing songs, but Isaiah's "heart throbs like a harp for Moab, and my very soul for Kirheres" (Isaiah 16:11). From the song of creation to the throbbing of Isaiah's heart, there exists a rhythm. It is in that rhythm that God's presence can be felt. God is there in the mountain's song to the heart beat of an individual.

There is a rhythm to life. We can see and hear and fear the rhythm of the flickering stars, the running gazelles, the splashing and dancing of dolphins, the song of the cricket, the flash of the lightning bug, the song of whales, the quiet whisper of a child, the fluttering of birds' wings rising out of the field, the beat of African drums, and the sound of the bass from a jazz quartet. We can hear the pounding of our own feet and that of others on the sidewalk, and if we listen closely, we can hear the rhythm in our chest.

The mystic rhythm is not intended to replace orthodoxy. Instead, it is a way of naming an attribute of God that is relevant to the 21st Century. It reinforces biblical orthodoxy. The mystic rhythm enhances an understanding of God. Standard Trinitarian orthodoxy must remain in place, but people need mystery that is relevant to the postmodern world. Something new and different must capture the human heart. Jesus turned over the tables in the Temple not to prove his humanity, but rather to express how the institutional Temple, its rules and regulations and practices, failed to create an environment open to God's desire for a new generation. The Pharisees could not feel the mystic rhythm. Today, the Church must be open to renewal, re-creation, and reformation in order to remain relevant to the people of a scientific age. This approach may help those who are searching find the Divine everywhere.

The real danger for the Church is when it allows science to co-opt the language of faith into a scientific belief system as in the case of Francis Collins' book, *The Language of God.* For Collins, science becomes the focal point of study not scripture. The knowledge of science increases and the understanding of Holy texts decrease. Again, religion is being co-opted by science. When the Church allows science to be the proof text for faith, then, faith runs the risk of being absorbed by science and no longer in touch with the Divine. Religion looses its identity through absorption into the dominant culture of technology and science. Religion and science need not be in war-like conflict. The two should be in an amiable conflict.

While touring the Natural Science Museum at the University of Oklahoma, a quote was etched on one of the walls. Professor Paul B. Sears wrote in 1935 these words, "Science has the power to illuminate, but not to solve the deeper problems of mankind. For always after knowledge come choice and action both of them intensely personal." Here is the role of faith, the Church, and religion. The Church is not in the business of explaining how the oceans were formed and how life came to be. Science, as a gift from God, brings forward knowledge of the natural world that helps us live better lives. This knowledge, however, does not prevent wars. Science may develop a way to address world hunger, but it takes compassionate people to make sure the starving people are fed. The Church can be the community to give voice and actions to a world in desperate need. Moral formation by the Church teaches that the first [those in positions of power] will be last and the last [the poor, marginalized] will be first. That is the story of hope.

The one religious trait that science cannot create in the lab is community. The Mystic Rhythm, as a Divine attribute, solidifies community by exposing the inter-connectedness of all things. All people have a rhythm to their heart beats and breathe rates as well as a rhythmic pattern to their walking strides. The myth allows for individuals and the community to move forward into an uncertain future. The myth provides the roots that help people resist whatever storms comes their way. Without it, we are helplessly tossed to and fro as the apostle Paul constantly reminds the Christian community. The myths of the past do not all translate into the present. Some myths are eternal, capturing the essence of human existence, but often, the myth must be told using the language of the day.

Science/technology creates false community—internet chat rooms, emailing, text messaging and so on. Techno-community does not provide an outlet for altruistic acts or "agape" love. In fact, one could argue that quite the contrary happens. Francis Collins is absolutely right when he says altruism is a major stumbling block for those who adhere to evolution. However, he is wrong in thinking that it some how exists in all of people. Paul writes in Romans 7 that his nature is not to do what is right but to do those things that are wrong, but it is by the grace of God carried out through community that he is able to practice agape or selfless love. Community teaches compassion.

Community is what separates faith from science and technology. People try to use technology in order to create community, but they fall short. Community is not just about text messaging back and forth. Community involves bringing soup to someone who has the flu. Community is about hugging a child just for the sake of hugging in order to express love by someone outside of the family. Community celebrates high school graduations. Community teaches moral and ethical behavior.

Religious community is more than corporate worship; it is also about intercession for one another or praying for one another while always reaching out in love to others in need and bringing them into the community. Pastor Bonhoeffer writes, "This brings us to a point at which we hear the *pulsing* [emphasis mine] of all Christian life in unison. A Christian fellowship lives and exists by the intercession of its members for one another, or it collapses. I can no longer condemn or hate a brother for whom I pray, no matter how much trouble he causes me. ... This makes it clear that intercession is also a daily service we owe to God and to our brother" (Bonhoeffer, 86). Christian community feels the Mystic Rhythm pulsating through its members, thus, driving each member of the community to reach out to another. If the Church fails to be an "intercessory community," it will collapse—like the bear—under its own weigh. The Church is on the ledge waiting to be pushed off by people substituting real, incarnate community for cyber space community. Real community fills the holes in people's lives. In some sense, God does fill the gaps, but it is the gap in the human heart yearning for meaning and desperately needing to be filled with the spirit of God and not smart phones and video games. People are desperately seeking meaning and fulfillment, so they enter chat rooms because the Church has not made itself relevant. They want relationships, so they join online dating arrangements or enter chat rooms. They want intimacy, so they seek pornographic websites. Conflicts are handled by email without seeing the person face to face. People say things they normally would not communicate from sexual flirtations to outright hatred and everything in between. Here lies the problem with technology. Today, expressions of love are text messaged. Here lies the problem with technology. By communicating one on one or within the cyber communities, chat rooms or blogging, people are unable to see the effect their words are having upon the other person. Sarcasm cannot be expressed by email or text messaging. This affects our ability to empathize. Sarcasm may be perceived as aggression. Friendship misconstrued as love and so forth. Only in real, flesh and blood community can the totality of human experience be felt and actualized. Technological community must be exchanged for authentic community which can use technology as a tool to enhance community. The Church must own up to its end of the bargain by creating a safe environment, developing true community based on honesty and transparency and carrying out Jesus' love ethic—love your neighbor as yourself.

For the Church to survive in the 21st Century, cultural and social relevancy is a must. Lose the relevancy and you lose several generations. The Church in the United States does not have time on its side. Its relevancy is directly challenged by science and technology. This conflict goes unnoticed because the Church is too fixated on the issues of gay clergy, abortion, and evolution vs. creationism. These are secondary issues that need to be addressed, but they do not pose a threat because in the postmodern era they simply are irrelevant to the majority of people under the age of forty-five—the Church's forgotten generation.

Science and technology do have far greater impact on faith in the 21st century than religion. Does this mean the Church should seek to eliminate science for its own survival? Of course not, science plays an important part in postmodern society. Science helps make the physical world a better place. The world needs new medicines, genetic research to eliminate diseases, alternative fuel sources, and beyond to quantum physics which helps us understand the complexity of the universe. As for people of belief, it affirms the beauty of Creation. The world also needs to hear the mystic rhythm which connects all of humanity. There are times when science and technology go too far, when it is co-opted by the industrial military complex. Without a unified Church or religion, who will step forward with a collective "No," when genetic research turns to genetic manipulations for the sake of controlling intelligence, eye color, body weight, and athleticism? The Church failed to say, "No," to Nazi Germany's sadistic and de-humanizing experimentations and attempts to create the perfect race. Here, science stepped way beyond its boundaries; a collective "No" by the church was needed even at great risk.

On the hand, the Church or religion must be careful that it, too, does not overstep its moral and ethical obligations when it separates, restricts, and prevents outsiders from joining the community. Religious communities must always seek out the stranger, the outsider, and the marginalized. When wars are carried out in the name of God, the Church or religion has overstepped its boundaries. When abortion doctors are shot or terrorists destroy buildings and take human life, religion has overstepped its boundaries.

Finally, the Church has three basic functions in our scientific, technologically-driven society to remain relevant in people's lives: First, it must provide authentic community where love and compassion are felt and expressed and shared with others inside the community as well as outside of it. Second, provide an alternative experience to a generation lost in cyber space and to those technological devices that keep people from one on one, flesh and blood relationships; and Three, science must be told, "No," on occasion. These define the role of the postmodern church. These will give it relevancy.

Church should not seek the elimination of science, and science should not seek the elimination of Church. Both mutually benefit one another when kept in an amiable conflict. Much literature has emerged from both science and religion calling seeking accommodation and unity. This is a mistake for both. When one accommodates the other, a level of identity is lost. Compromise is not necessarily beneficial. When two parties reach a compromise, each one must give up something. Conflict between Church and science needs to exist, but that conflict does not mean destruction. The healthiest relationship between Church and science is an amiable conflict; whereas, both can argue, critique, and debate issues of moral and ethical-ramifications. Conflict can be amiable, and when understood in this way, great creativity can emerge. Non-destructive conflict births creativity. Creation came out of conflict— God encountered the primordial waters. In regards to its relationship to society and science, the Church must be the "resident acquaintance" with one foot in the hereafter and the other one firmly planted in society offering the world not just salvation but a better place to live guided by community living out Jesus' love ethic—that there is no greater love than to lay down one's life for a brother or sister. Science/technology should make people's physical lives better. The Church/religion brings meaning to their lives. Trouble exists when science becomes sacred and mythological and when theology becomes secular. Science exceeds its limits when data and discoveries are used to annihilate teachings about God, or to be identified with God. In addition, Science should not seek to solve all humanity's problems even the existential ones. On the other hand, theology is secularized when it rejects its character and role in the world as well as its eschatological nature. Theology's greatest temptation is to use scientific methodology to describe God.

The cosmic christology [understanding of Christ] of the ancient world "confronted Christ the redeemer with a world of powers, spirits, and gods. The proclamation of 'universal reconciliation' freed believers from their fear of the world and from their terror of demons. Today a cosmic christology has to confront Christ the redeemer with a nature which humans have plunged into chaos, infected with poisonous waste and condemned to universal death, so that he can save men and women from their despair and nature from annihilation" (Moltmann, 89).

One last word to the 21st century Church, stop reading Holy Scripture as static, frozen in time, and never changing. God reveals himself in different ways for each generation. God's word is alive and adaptive. Scripture itself provides the best reason. Deuteronomy 23:1 states, "No one whose testicles are crushed or whose penis is cut off shall be admitted to the assembly of the Lord." Of course, this is a direct reference to the eunuchs. Several centuries later, the prophet Isaiah writes, "For thus says the Lord: To the eunuchs who keep my Sabbaths, who choose the things that please me and hold fast my covenant, I will give, in my house and within in my walls, a monument and a name better than sons and daughters; I will give them an everlasting name that shall not be cut off" (Isaiah 56:4-5). Several centuries later, Luke writes in Acts 8:38, "He commanded the chariot to stop, and both of them, Philip and the eunuch, went down into the water, and Philip baptized him."

There is a rhythm to life that permeates all things. Each song is sung or played differently for each generation. All humanity has to do is hear it. It is heard in community—something science cannot provide. In a church, there were two sisters who lived together and cared for each for forty years. They had no living family and minimal income. They were both in their nineties. The older sister dies leaving the younger one alone. Science could not stop the cancer; it could go no further. The sisters were faithful members of the church for seventy-seven years. Their church community stepped in where science could go no further. The remaining sister is under the care of the church. Text messaging, e-mailing, cyber cafes, and so forth cannot deliver chicken soup or check for depression among the elderly.

Notes

All biblical references come from the New Revised Standard Version, *The New Oxford Annotated Bible*, Eds. Bruce M. Metzger and Roland E. Murphy, New York: Oxford Press, 1989.

Chapter 1:

1. John Updike, *Villages*, (New York: Ballantine Books, 2004), 308.
2. Associated Press, *Arkansas Democrat-Gazette*, (December 22, 2007), 4B.
3. Ibid, 4B.
4. John F. Haught, "Restoring Our Sense of Belonging," *Ecology, Cosmology, and Theology: A Trialogue,"* (*Woodstock Report,* June 1994, no. 38), 3-10.
5. Religious Tolerance. Org. "Trends Among Christians in the US," http://www.religioustolerance.org/chr_tren.htm, (November 4, 2007).

6.   Jon Meacham, "The End of Christian America," *Newsweek*, (April 13, 2009), 34.

7.   Pope John Paul II, "Science and Human Values," *L'Osservatore Romano*, (July 15, 1985), *Marcel Grossman Meeting on Relativistic Astrophysics* in June 21, 1985.

8.   Ibid, 1-2.

9.   Brad Igou, "Amish Country News," *Amish Country News Publisher* (December 3, 2002) 1.

10. Pope John Paul II, "Science Serves Humanity Only When It Is Joined to Conscience," *L'Osservatore Romano*, (January 22, 1997), *International Conference on Space Research*, January 11, 1997.

11. Stanley Hauerwas, *With the Grain of the Universe*, (Grand Rapids: Brazos Press, 2001), 29.

12. Ibid, 37-38.

13. Pope John Paul II, "Science and Faith in the Search for Truth," *L'Osservatore Romano* (November 15, 1980), Web publishing with permission by the Newman Center at California Institute of Technology.

14. Ibid, 2.

15. Hauerwas, 29.

16. Ibid, 32.

17. Justos L. Gonzales, *The Story of Christianity, vol. 2,* (San Francisco: HarperSanFrancisco press, *1985*), 185.

18. Ibid, 186.

19. Ibid, 187-188.

20. Ibid, 189.

21. Ibid, 189.

22. Ibid, 190.

23. Ibid, 192.

24. Ibid, 194-95

25. Ibid, 361-64.

26. Paul Stroble, *What About Science and Religion?* (Nashville: Abingdon Press, 2007), 48.

27. Kenneth Cauthen, "Science and Technology," (Kenneth Cauthen, 2000), 1-10.

28. *Arkansas Democrat-Gazette*, 4B.

29. Pope John Paul (Nov., 1980), 1-2.

Chapter 2:

1.   John Updike, *Rabbit, Run,* (New York: Fawcet Crest, 1960),
     142.
2.   Jeffery Johnson, "Updike's Passions," *The Christian Century,*
     (March 24, 2009), 12.
3.   Jurgen Moltmann, *Jesus Christ for Today's World,* (Minneapolis:
     Fortress Press, 1994), 88.
4.   Ibid, 88
5.   Ibid, 89
6.   Hannah Arendt, "The Conquest of Space and the Stature of
     Man." *Between Past and Future,* (New York: Penguin Books,
     LTD, 1954), 276.
7.   Ibid, 278
8.   Dean Doner, "Rabbit Angstrom's Unseen World." *New World
     Writing,* 20(1962), 18. Rpt. in John Updike: A Collection of
     Critical Essays, (Englewood Clifts: Prentice-Hall, 1979).
9.   *Rabbit, Run*, 94.
10. Ibid, 15
11. Ibid, 15
12. Ibid, 15
13. Ibid, 28
14. Ibid, 37
15. Ibid, 39
16. Ibid, 39
17. Doner, 26
18. *Rabbit, Run*, 45
19. Ibid, 53
20. Ibid, 119
21. Ibid, 108
22. Ibid, 139
23. Ibid, 142
24. Ibid, 142
25. Ibid, 142
26. Ibid, 35

27. Ibid, 182
28. Ibid, 160
29. Arendt, 265
30. Ibid, 265-66
31. *Rabbit, Run*, 183
32. Ibid, 187
33. Doner, 23
34. *Rabbit, Run*, 208
35. Ibid, 269
36. Doner, 32
37. Ibid, 32
38. *Rabbit, Run*, 152
39. Ibid, 272
40. Ibid, 266
41. Ibid, 273
42. Arendt, 278-79
43. Ibid, 274-76
44. *Rabbit, Run* 282-83
45. Ibid, 284
46. Ibid, 40
47. Ibid, 260
48. Ibid, 260
49. Ibid, 71
50. Ibid, 126
51. Ibid, 127
52. Ibid, 85
53. Ibid, 126
54. John Updike, *Rabbit Redux*, (New York: Fawcett Crest, 1971), 13.
55. Ibid, 16
56. Ibid, 17
57. Charles Berryman, "The Education of Harry Angstrom: Rabbit and the Moon," *The Literary Review*, 27(1983), 119.
58. *Rabbit Redux*, 122
59. Ibid, 21
60. Ibid, 26
61. Arendt, 265-280

62. *Rabbit Redux,* 28
63. Ibid, 32
64. W.F. Hilton, *Manned Satellites,* (New York: Harper and Row Publishers, 1965), 35-37.
65. *Rabbit Redux, 32*
66. Ibid, 40
67. Ibid, 41
68. Ibid, 45
69. Ibid, 55
70. Ibid, 70
71. Ibid, 70
72. Ibid, 73
73. Ibid, 81
74. Ibid, 86
75. Ibid, 121
76. Ibid, 143
77. Ibid, 144
78. Ibid, 144
79. Ibid, 152
80. Ibid, 208
81. Ibid, 211
82. Edward M. Jackson, "Rabbit Is Racist," *CLA Journal*, 28(1984-85), ed. Cason L. Hill, 444.
83. *Rabbit Redux*, 221
84. Ibid, 296-97
85. Ibid, 297
86. Ibid, 269
87. Ibid, 318
88. Ibid, 332
89. Ibid, 338
90. Robert Detweiller, *John Updike,* (New York: Twayne Publishers, Inc, 1972), 155.
91. Ibid, 155
92. *Rabbit Redux,* 19
93. Ibid, 23
94. Ibid, 58
95. Ibid, 276

96. Ibid, 281
97. Ibid, 62
98. Ibid, 69-70
99. Ibid, 84
100. Ibid, 111
101. John Updike, *Rabbit Is Rich.* (New York: Alfred A. Knopf, 1981), 3.
102. Ibid, 10
103. Ibid, 6
104. Ibid, 3
105. Ibid, 7
106. Ibid, 13
107. Ibid, 22
108. Ibid, 34
109. Ibid, 46
110. Ibid, 50
111. Ibid, 62
112. Ibid, 75
113. Ibid, 79
114. Ibid, 82
115. Ibid, 94
116. Ibid, 96
117. Ibid, 98
118. Ibid, 104
119. Ibid, 105
120. Ibid, 106
121. Ibid, 107
122. Ibid, 134
123. Ibid, 138
124. Ibid, 139
125. Ibid, 139
126. Ibid, 141
127. Ibid, 177
128. Ibid, 177
129. Ibid, 178
130. Ibid, 4
131. Ibid, 12

132. Ibid, 29
133. Ibid, 188
134. Ibid, 189
135. Ibid, 191
136. Ibid, 226
137. Ibid, 229
138. Ibid, 232
139. Ibid, 271
140. Ibid, 305
141. Ibid, 417
142. Ibid, 467
143. John Updike, *Rabbit At Rest,* (New York: Alfred A. Knopf, 1990), 3.
144. Ibid, 5
145. Ibid, 6
146. Ibid, 8-9
147. Ibid, 12
148. Ibid, 14
149. Ibid, 23
150. Ibid, 44
151. Ibid, 50
152. Ibid, 56
153. Ibid, 72
154. Ibid, 76
155. Ibid, 78
156. Ibid, 83
157. Ibid, 85
158. Ibid, 98
159. Ibid, 103
160. Ibid, 103
161. Ibid, 105
162. Ibid, 110
163. Ibid, 115
164. Ibid, 127
165. Ibid, 145
166. Ibid, 171
167. Ibid, 174

168. Ibid, 127
169. Ibid, 181
170. Ibid, 181
171. Ibid, 181
172. Ibid, 184
173. Ibid, 185
174. Ibid, 188
175. Ibid, 219
176. Ibid, 231
177. Ibid, 264
178. Ibid, 281
179. Ibid, 326
180. Ibid, 327
181. Ibid, 345
182. Ibid, 346
183. Ibid, 358
184. Ibid, 363
185. Ibid, 370-71
186. Ibid, 411-13
187. Ibid, 413
188. Ibid, 432
189. Ibid, 444
190. Ibid, 457
191. Ibid, 469
192. Ibid, 479
193. Ibid, 487
194. *Rabbit, Run,* 9
195. *Rabbit At Rest,* 512
196. John Updike, *Toward the End of Time,* (New York: Fawcett Books, 1997), 34.
197. Ibid, 116
198. Ibid, 151-52
199. Ibid, 152
200. *Villages,* 198
201. Ibid, 199
202. Ibid, 271

Chapter 3:

1. Robert Jastrow, Robert Park, Margaret Wertheim, John Haught, "Collision Between Science and Religion," Ben Wattenberg. *Think Tank,* PBS, May 16, 2006, www.pbs.org/thinktank, 1-3.

2. Robert Wright, *The Moral Animal,* (New York: Vintage Books, 1994), 160-61.

3. Hauerwas, 23-24

4. Francis S. Collins, *The Language of God,* (New York: Free Press, 2006), 49.

5. Ibid, 51

6. Jurgen Moltmann, *Jesus Christ for Today's World,* (Minneapolis, 1994), 88-90.

7. Ibid, 90

8. Ibid, 90

9. Ibid, 90

10. David Van Biema, "God VS Science," *Time Magazine* (November 13, 2006), 53-54.

11. Collins, 66

12. Ibid, 66

13. Dietrich Bonhoeffer, *Ethics,* (New York: Simon & Schuster, 1995), 201.

14. Dietrich Bonhoeffer, *The Cost of Discipleship,* (New York: Touchstone, 1995), 116-17.

15. Haught, 2

16. Pope John Paul II, "Faith Can Never Conflict with Reason," *L'Osservatore Romano,* (November 4, 1992), 1-2

17. Ibid, 4-5

18. Ibid, 5

19. United Methodist News Service, "Church Opposes Cloning of Humans to Produce Babies," *Arkansas United Methodist,* (February, 1 2008), 1.

20. Pope John Paul II, 1992, 5.

21. Pope John Paul II, "Science Serves Humanity Only When It Is Joined to Conscience," *Catholic Information Network*, (January 22, 1997), 1.
22. Ibid, 2
23. Pope John Paul II, "The Problems of Science are the Problems of Man," *L'Osservatore Romano*, (April 3, 1979, vol. 12, n. 14), 2.
24. Ibid, 2
25. Ibid, 2
26. Pope John Paul II, "The Human Person Must Be the Beginning Subject and Goal of All Scientific Research," *L'Osservatore Romano*, weekly edition, (November 9, 1994).
27. Pope John Paul II, 1979, 2.
28. Biema, 50
29. Heather Hahn, "Fisher of Men Uses Net to Reach Out to Worshippers," *Arkansas Democrat-Gazette*, 2 February, 2008, 6B.
30. John Neustadt, MD, "Fracture Proof Your Bone," *Bottom Line.* (June 1, 2008, vol. 30, no. II), 1.
31. Cauthen, 2
32. Cauthen, 4
33. Bonhoeffer, *Life Together,* 100
34. *Think Tank*, 2
35. Pope John Paul II, 1994, 1
36. Beima, 50
37. Beima, 50

Chapter 4:

1. *Think Tank, 3*
2. John Jefferson Davis, "Theological Reflections on Chaos Theory," *Perspectives on Science and Christian Faith*, 49, (June, 1997), 1-3.
3. Dave Ussery, "The Purpose-Driven *iPod*," *The Christian Century,* (September 23, 2008), 11.
4. Ibid, 4
5. Ibid, 4

6. Ibid, 4
7. Ibid, 4-5
8. Ibid, 3-4
9. Ibid, 5
10. Ibid, 6
11. Ibid, 6-7
12. Ibid, 7
13. Ibid, 9
14. Sjord L. Bonting, "Chaos Theory Revisted," http://home-1. tiscali.nl/-sttdc/bontingtheology.htm, 1999, 1-3.
15. Ibid, 2-4
16. Moltmann, 100-01
17. Neal Magee, "Determinism, Total Predictability, and the Uncertainty Principle in Chaotic Systems: Theological Implications," TH417, J. Wentzel van Huyssteen (fall, 1994), 6.
18. Bonting, 1
19. Ibid, 2
20. Ibid, 2
21. Ibid, 3

Chapter 5:
1. "Albert Einstein's Quotes on Spirituality," *Judaism Online.* simpletoremember.com.
2. Gregory Stock. "Choosing Our Genes." *The Futurist,* (July-August, 2002), 19.
3. *Futurist,* 35-39
4. *Toward the End of Time,* 232
5. Moltmann, 96
6. Brian Green, *The Elegant Universe,* (New York: Vintage Books, 2003), 135.
7. Moltmann, 96
8. Mark Morford, "How to Sing Like a Planet," *SFGate.com,* 23 April, 2008.
9. Morford, 3
10. Moltmann, 89

Works Cited In the Text

Arendt, Hannah. "The Conquest of Space and the Stature of Man." *Between Past And Future*. New York: Penguin Books LTD, 1954.

Associated Press. *Arkansas Democrat-Gazette*. 22 Dec. 2007, 4B.

Berryman, Charles. "The Education of Harry Angstrom: Rabbit and the Moon." *The*

Literary Review, 27 (1983) pp. 117-26.

Biema, David Van. "God vs. Science." *Time Magazine*. 13 Nov. 2006: 53-54.

Bonhoeffer, Dietrich. *The Cost of Discipleship*. New York: Simon & Schuster, 1995.

_____. *Ethics*. New York: Simon & Schuster, 1995.

Bonting, Sjord L. "Chaos Theory Revisted." http//www.bontingtheology. htm, 1999.

Cauthen, Kenneth. "Science and Technology." http//www.frontiernet. net, 2000.

Collins, Francis. *The Language of God.* New York: Free Press, 2006.

Davis, John Jefferson. "Theological Reflections on Chaos Theory." *Perspectives on*

Science and Christian Faith. 49 (June, 1997). Pp. 1-3.

Detweiller, Robert. *John Updike.* New York: Twayne Publishers, Inc, 1972.

Doner, Dean. "Rabbit Angstrom's Unseen World." *New World Writing.* 20(1962): 63-75.

Rpt. in *John Updike: A Collection Of Critical Essays.* Eds. David Thorburn and Howard Eiland. Englewood Clifts: Prentice-Hall, 1979.

Gonzales, Justos L. *The Story of Christianity, vol. 2.* San Francisco: HarperSanFrancisco Press, 1985.

Green, Brian. *The Elegant Universe.* New York: Vintage Books, 2003.

Hahn, Heather. "Fisher of Men Uses Net to Reach Out to Worshippers."

Arkansas Democrat-Gazette 28 March 2009, 4B.

Haught, John F. "Restoring Our Sense of Belonging." *Woodstock Report,* 38 (June, 1994): pp. 3-10.

Hauerwas, Stanley. *With the Grain of the Universe.* Grand Rapids: Brazos Press, 2001.

Hilton, W.F. *Manned Satellites.* New York: Harper and Row Publishers, 1965.

Igou, Brad. "Amish Country News." *Amish Country News Publisher* December 2002: pg. 1.

Jackson, Edward. "Rabbit Is Racist." CLA Journal, 28.(1984-85) Ed. Cason L. Hill.

Jastrow, Robert, Robert Park, Margaret Wertheim, John Haught. "Collision Between

Science and Religion." Think Tank PBS 12 May 2006.

Johnson, Jeffery. "Updike's Passions." *The Christian Century*, March, 2009: pg. 12.

Magee, Neal. "Determinism, Total Predictability, and the Uncertainty Principle in

Chaotic Systems: Theological Implications." TH417, J. Wentzel Van Huyssteen, Fall 1994.

Moltmann, Jurgen. *Jesus Christ for Today's World*. Minneapolis: Fortress Press, 1994.

Morford, Mark. "How to Sing Like a Planet." *SFGate.com*, April 2008.

Meacham, Jon. "The End of Christian America." *Newsweek* 13 April 2009: pp. 34-38

Neustadt, John. "Facture Proof Your Bone." *Bottom Line* 30, II June 2008: pg. 1.

Paul, Pope John. "Faith Can Never Conflict With Reason." *L'Osservatore Romano* 4 Nov. 1992.

_____. "The Human Person Must Be the Beginning Subject and Goal of All Scientific

Research." *L'Osservatore Romano* 9 November 1994.

_____. "The Problems of Science are the Problems of Man." *L'Osservatore Romano* 3 April 1979.

_____. "Science and Faith in Search for Truth." *L'Osservatore Romano* 22 January 1980.

_____. "Science and Human Values." *L'Osservatore Romano* 15 July 1985.

_____. "Science Serves Humanity Only When It Is Joined to Conscience." *Catholic Information Network* 22 January 1997.

Religious Tolerance.Org. "Trends Among Christians in the US." www.religioustolerance.org 4 November 2007: pp. 1-3.

Stock, Gregory. "Choosing Our Genes." *The Futurist* July-August 2002: pp. 19, 35-39.

Strobble, Paul. *What About Science and Religion?* Nashville: Abingdon Press, 2007.

Updike, John. *Rabbit, Run.* New York: Fawcett Crest, 1960.

_____. *Rabbit Redux.* New York: Fawcett Crest, 1971.

_____. *Rabbit Is Rich.* New York: Alfred A. Knopf, 1981.

_____. *Rabbit At Rest.* New York: Alfred A. Knopf, 1990.

Ussery, David. "The Purpose-Driven *iPod*." *The Christian Century* 23 Sept. 2008: Pg. 11.

Wright, Robert. 1994. *The Moral Animal.* New York: Vintage Books.